D1292859

# THE SOCIAL STUDIES:
*Myths and Realities*

# THE
# SOCIAL STUDIES
*Myths and Realities*

by DAVID F. KELLUM

A SEARCH BOOK: SHEED AND WARD
NEW YORK

*For Chrissie,*
*Dave and Sam*

# PREFACE

Strictly speaking, this isn't a methods text. I hate them. There are no sample lesson plans included in these pages. Lesson plans can be bought in quantity from commercial outlets by any teacher faced with the prospect of having to offer a course and knowing nothing about it. In these pages you will find included an essay that undertakes to treat of the nature of a lesson plan, what it is, why it is, and how one goes about constructing one. It is this, rather, that is the character of the book: a consideration of how and why people teach social studies—not what to teach.

I had considered including some samples of teaching devices that I had constructed; but rejected the idea on the grounds that in providing such I would be doing no service to the teachers who are convinced that they need them, and a positive disservice to the students whom they victimize. In any event there are available great three or four-pound affairs that have all this sort of thing that many teachers seem to need, or think they need—sample unit plans, models, graphs and all the latest. Such texts exist in such numbers that I am haunted by the fear that great teachers will insist ahead of time that they have neither the time nor the patience to read through this effort either. I hope not. I'm confident that this is different, and that it's worth reading.

This is a sassy book—it even fights. It has fought with me and I suspect it will fight with you. I have excluded two chapters that did appear in the early drafts, one suggesting the latent power of high school students with which we as teachers were going to have to reckon (which is even now pushing itself into view), and one suggesting the general hopelessness of our teacher preparation programs.

I know that the pages that are here contain contradictions. There are contradictions in teaching. There are ideas set forth in these essays which I have challenged myself upon re-reading. As this appears in print, I will have re-espoused some of them and rejected others. This does not disturb me, because I consider it part of the normal process of growth. I have neither the time nor the interest to sit behind a desk and chart maps for the educational universe. Undoubtedly, inconsistencies are much more fearsome things in the rarified atmosphere of the grand designers. I have to meet classes five days a week.

# CONTENTS

# THE SOCIAL STUDIES:
*Myths and Realities*

# ONE

## WHY ANOTHER BOOK ON TEACHING SOCIAL STUDIES?

Books related to education rarely have any discernible impact on anything. Even Immanuel Kant's textbook on pedagogy written after years of his own teaching experience has not become part of any corporate body of systematic thought as one might have expected. In fact, it was disowned by its author. Why? The chief reason is that every teacher, good or bad, is an island unto himself. Teachers operate independently of, and often oblivious to, professional literature. This, it develops with some reading in the field, is among the choicest of God's blessings upon them. But so it happens that the things that we know and the things that we discover as individual teachers through the experience of teaching never find their way into *corpus scientiae*. The massive challenges that have already broken the surface and which pose the need of total reorganization of our instructional programs—both in terms of their content and teaching methods—have successfully eluded any collective notice of the profession as a whole. For the profession is not a whole; neither is it a profession.

Instead, the new challenges will be met, as in the past, sporadically and by the independent efforts and resources of the individual classroom teachers, thousands of them. However, many of our thousands of classroom teachers will not be able to cope; indeed much of our curriculum and many of our teachers have already slipped into an obscure but comfortable obsolescence. Some have been there for years and years. The result is that, discounting instances of bold and inspired instruction brought into play by isolated visionaries often operating on scant salaries, the gap between the demands of the 21st century and our horse-and-buggy instruction widens into a grotesquerie. We lack the capacity for organized response as a profession to problems that confront all of us because we recognize them only as individual problems. More than this, collective recognition of the problems would be no guarantee of collective action on them. Certainly, given the teachers' individualism, no book will accomplish either of these results. But this, for reasons to be explored shortly, is neither unnatural nor necessarily catastrophic.

Beyond this, comment on contemporary social studies instruction practices—particularly comment that takes the form of indictment—is irrelevant because the present challenges are of such dimensions as to demand action that ranges far beyond a mere salvaging operation. The forces now looming before us suggest the necessity of reconstructing our entire education program on altogether different and largely unfamiliar bases. It becomes increasingly obvious that the schools of 1985 will bear little resemblance to those with which we are dealing at present.

The number of people who earn livings as classroom teachers will level within a generation and then drop sharply. The role of the teacher will be drastically altered from that of principal source of instruction to that of source gatherer and research director, much more closely akin to our current librarian than to our remembered school marm. The simple fact is that our mass communication media easily out-teach the best of us.

Even now the haunting suspicion lurks that in areas serviced by responsible radio and television programming, the child learns much more by staying home sick than he does by going to school.

Classrooms will disappear—as even now the tendency of the modern school buildings is toward fewer and fewer walls— to be replaced by research and audio-visual centers. Public libraries are already more appropriate as centers of learning and the modifications necessary to enable them to meet mass needs are both technically simple and comparatively inexpensive. The momentum toward research or source centers will be swelled by growing public dissatisfaction with rising school costs and what the public often correctly identifies as "frills." To the public and to the teacher, the writing on the wall is plain: one hour of carefully prepared television programming easily outdistances a week of schoolroom work in terms of effective and genuine learning experience.

The definition of public education will be expanded to include the public rather than simply the public's children. The problem of the drop-out will be dwarfed by the problem of the drop-in, as standard school programs merge with adult education programs which in several very important respects are vastly more appropriate means to fulfill our commitment to mass education. The curriculum will be completely overhauled and assume more and more the dimensions of the adult education curriculum, leaving *ratio studiorum* further and further behind.

Certainly the changes will be basic and sweeping, and their radical nature will be emphasized by the speed with which they force themselves upon us, by the fact that we have not collectively anticipated nor provided for them, and by the fact that great numbers of teachers are not disposed either intellectually or temperamentally to meet them.

Then why another book on teaching social studies? I suppose

that the book is written for me, a catharsis for an overwrought teacher who wants to stretch out his hand in the dark and reassure himself that his fellow teachers are still there.

(Still purging): I suppose that for all of the complaints that are leveled at methods texts, what's actually wrong with them can be reduced to two basic things: the people who write them and the people who read them. I began teaching a methods course in social studies at Columbia Teachers College in 1962 and my search for substantial comment on the subject has grown so desperate that I undertake constructing one of my own. I approach this with the quiet confidence that I am no writer; but, having explored dozens of existent texts, I am encouraged that effective communication is not necessarily a prerequisite. Certainly this effort can be no worse than what is already available to teachers.

In fact I am heartened by two things: first, I believe that, contrary to an impression formed from a viewing of available texts, there are some worthwhile ideas to be considered; second, I am a teacher. I know this because the janitors don't like me. The distinction between teachers and the people who write about teaching is both basic and unavoidable. I am exhausted by the twaddle produced by professional pedagooks who themselves could not run a forty-two minute study hall, much less turn in a creditable performance in a high school social studies class. But forgive my disenchantment.

The experienced classroom teacher could not seriously entertain for any length of time the illusion under which the text author works from the first. The methods textbook's existence is rooted in the premise that literate human beings can be taught how to teach; that the act of effective teaching can somehow be reduced to a body of do's and don't's, a handful of "neat" ideas, and (not surprising in this day and age), to a series of mathematical formulae which can be projected on a pair of X and Y axes. The acceptance of this premise is rarely, if ever, challenged. Indeed the weight of our entire teacher preparation program at the college and university level rests upon the same basic notion—that effective teaching is basically scientific. And so we arm the students in our methods courses with texts on the subject and then provide objective tests at the end of the semester to discover how well they've learned. Unhappily the notion is for the greater part false. The discouraging truth of the matter is that teachers are born, not made. All literates cannot be taught how to teach; I doubt very much that anyone can. And the truth of the matter persists though we crowd it into the back of our minds to make ourselves more comfortable in the face of a vast economic commitment to elaborate teacher training programs and textbooks. As a methods teacher, I find the idea especially haunting and distressing, but the fact remains that teaching is not learnable; teaching is not a science. Much, if not most, of our teacher education thinking and practice is an act of faith in what is pure and simple alchemy.

But the notion that teaching is a science is implicit in the pages of the methods text, and the implicit agreement of writer and reader in that notion is one of the great misfortunes of the teaching world. Yet once beyond the walls of the university with its education courses and its textbooks, its credit hours and its great theories of learning and scholarly research, once beyond all of this and into one's own classroom with the door closed, we are struck by the steadily growing realization (which apparently does not wither even in the face of renewed course work later on) that teaching is an art. The teacher is an artist. He may be a great artist or a poor one, or a mediocre one (which is the most painful), but he is an artist. And it is a world worth waiting for. To be sure, there will be more conventions from time to time at which he will be required to pay proper respect to the latest models and graphs which plot for him what great teaching is and show him how it works. But at last in the classroom and on salary he is free to work his art.

As in the case of any other artist, the teacher confronts and must solve two major problems: the problem of synthesis and the problem of communication. So, incidentally, does a telegraph operator, the major difference being that the success or failure of the teacher's synthesis and communication depends finally upon his personality. For the telegraph operator, nothing depends upon personality and everything depends upon his technical skill. In many ways the methods course would have been more appropriate to his line. It is because so much of the teacher's success depends upon the imagination with which he synthesizes and the individuality of his expression, that he properly considers himself an island. He resents the notion of the "right way" and the "wrong way" of teaching, and rejects the notion of general laws applicable to all teachers. The idea that all that he does and can do can be "researched" drives him to distraction. The lamentable gap that exists between our classroom teachers and our university education programs is the result of our inability to close with this proper understanding of the essential nature of teaching.

The "capital E" education problem is familiar to all classroom teachers and is the subject of much of their most strident criticism: that the courses they are taking or have taken, and the books they are required to read are hopelessly theoretical and without necessary application to anything real or alive. The peculiar character of education instruction, whether it takes the form of course lecture or textbook, is that it is obvious and naive. Perhaps more disconcerting is the attempt to camouflage this laborious exposition of the obvious with the invention and circulation of an inane pseudo-scientific jargon.

The problem is expanded by a repetitious and tired thoughtlessness both in text and lectures that might have inspired Luigi Pirandello to describe it as discourse in search of a subject. The inevitable result is that both texts and courses swell to an absurd length, while the principal lesson to be taught to any teacher is to say what you have to say and no more. Alas, in the course of their training they receive no salutary example except a lecture or two on the subject.

Compounding the difficulties of anemic content, sterile theoretics, bogus "research," the hopelessly naive, the profoundly obscure and the magnificently obvious, the professional literature sets it all forth in a Dick and Jane style that would offend the literary sensibilities of a sixth grader and that the adult mind should find intolerable.

Reverting to theory is the natural tendency of those who have little or no luck with practice; but the artist, however unhappily, needs practice. By and large those who are charged with, or who have appointed themselves to, greatest responsibility for the encouragement and refinement of the art of teaching, that is, textbook authors and those people who offer course instruction to other people on how to teach, are themselves artless people. Some of the methods instructors I have personally sampled and some I have seen other students subjected to, were themselves classically ineffective teachers, and I suspect in some instances even ineffective people. The two, obviously, are by no means unrelated. Collectively there are enough such people writing books and giving courses to convert the field of education finally into an intellectual Sahara and the laughing stock of the university and of the North American continent.

This then is the picture of the teacher training environment familiar to today's teacher. It simply should not be. And it need not be. As a teacher I abhor it.

To say that teaching is an art, however, is not to say that there is no legitimate need for some technical instruction for prospective teachers and no need for further attention to the problems of the practicing classroom teacher. The point is that what is being done is being done badly and on so wide a scale as to assume the proportions of an all-inclusive charade.

A *good* methods course or a *good* methods text would be a God-send. There is need of methods instruction for teachers just as there is need for formal training for any artist. The danger lies in misrepresenting the importance of technique, which instruction can provide, and talent, which instruction cannot provide. Yet we consistently misrepresent their relative importance. One of the most important contributors to this misplaced emphasis is the teaching license requirements established in the various states and provinces. We admit teachers to the classroom on the basis of their accumulated credit hours with utter disregard of talent. There is no process by which we may evaluate the qualitative aspect. (This lack of control over teacher certification, incidentally, is another index to the disparity between the terms "teacher" and "profession.") The finest instruction in technique possible—which we don't have— is wasted where there is no native talent for teaching. Assuming talent, effective instruction in technique then involves substantive comment. Such comment should be (a) informed (b) informative and (c) readable. Most available methods texts are (d) none of these.

Far too much of our comment is theoretical. Informed comment on the art of teaching and the development of teaching technique must be based upon more than theoretics propounded by drawing board specialists; it must be based somehow and somewhere upon successful classroom experience. The quality of being informed must include the concept of usefulness. Theories generated by *a priori* reasoning may be perfectly sound, but again they may not. In the instance of instruction in technique there is little time to be spent on "notions." To be useful, the emphasis must be upon the practical. Courses in counterpoint and harmony are of little use to a would-be musician who can't reproduce them for himself and apply the principles in constructing a composition. The practical applications of theory must be at once apparent—or immediately at hand—to those instructed. We have allowed a divorce between theory and practice, and we are permitting it to widen.

I am not urging that theory has no place in instruction. Over a period of time experience will generate theory. Such theory does have value because it can be re-converted into practice, assuming that it has been reproduced intact. Moreover, in its theory form it provides a basis for other modifications and variations resulting in a constantly expanding classroom efficacy.

Among the problems connected with the uses of theory is that what works for one teacher does not necessarily work for others; more vexing, what works for one teacher in the third period class does not work for the same teacher in the sixth period class. Theory once born (to theorize for a moment) tends to move away from the experience which generated it in search of wider and wider application. The good methods text will constantly correct for this tendency and make students aware of it, as well as keeping theory viable by constantly re-applying it. When we lose sight of applications and come to deal only with theoretics, we are no longer adequately informed.

There are several great variables operating in the classroom that mitigate against the construction of air-tight theory, finally making it impossible. We are not chemists or physicists. While the teaching world has paid tremendous tribute to science and has worked desperately during this century to reproduce its methods and results, it is probably closer to the truth to admit that we need a separate theory for every teacher and for every student—an unexciting prospect for those of us who yearn for the immutable truth. But the classroom teacher is confronted, nevertheless, with a need for some thirty individual theories per class. Bearing in mind these individual differences and the fact that the teacher is in a much better position to calculate his own particular needs and those of his students, an informative comment ventured by one teacher to another is appropriately left incomplete. Propriety—to say nothing of modesty—requires that only the dimensions of possibilities as possibilities should be advanced by the text in the hope that the teacher in Edmonton, Alberta and another in Sarasota, Florida may give them form and apply them to their unique situations. Few such comments are so constructed or advanced. Their nature tends to be proscriptive, settling all questions for all teachers for all times. Except by a stroke of fantastic coincidence then, the teacher who depends upon such proscription (aside from being an unimaginative soul and woefully ineffective) is likely to be constantly bewildered.

Among the teachers who cannot cope today and will not be able to cope tomorrow are all those dismal creatures who pore over methods texts and the writings of other teachers in search of an idea, the key that will unlock great pedagogy to them, too. As stated before, half of what's wrong with methods texts are the people who read them. When a new text appears offering a "new" method, the educational world rocks while the theorists and their sycophants try to discover what they've been doing so that they can reject that, re-tool, and undertake the general reorganization of everything that everyone else has been thinking.

One methods' comment on my book shelf states unequivocally that the inquiry approach is the only defensible way to teach social studies. Now there's nothing wrong with the inquiry method—in fact, for some teachers it's a most useful and exciting possibility. All that's wrong with the approach is that it was unfortunate enough to have attracted the attention of disciples like the author of this comment, who then spread the gospel to the waiting mindless—a species of intellectual parasitism. As far as the breakthrough idea is concerned, of course, the inquiry approach is no newer than Socrates. But when a new book championing the latest theory appears, my office is deluged with phone calls from panting spokesmen for teacher organizations asking that I appear before their group and explain it to them. The teachers are gathered in a meeting, and with no little embarrassment, I try to say something that will be useful to the one or two real teachers who might be among them. The rest don't care what's said, but they do respond knowingly to a liberal sprinkling of big names from the world of pedagookery; so I oblige by saying erudite things like "Taba," "Bruner," or "Wesleyanwronski." It's all very grand. Generally I quote two figures for speaking engagements: the lower one for straight speeches and a higher one which includes distribution of materials. Usually I find that when it comes to education, money is no object; people want the works.

Unable to help many then, I would introduce this essay only to those classroom or prospective classroom teachers who are accustomed to doing a good deal of their own thinking. Presented here is a collection, or more aptly a morass, of unfinished thoughts awaiting a reader. I apologize in advance for whatever dogmatism may creep in. There's bound to be some. For teachers this is an occupational hazard. Certainly none of the answers are here, but perhaps a few of the questions—questions that have arisen in my own teaching—are.

A final note: like you, I have known a good many classroom teachers who were exceptionally authoritarian in their approach to teaching, who "ran tight ships," and who conducted rather "formal" classes. Many were, and are, extremely effective and admirable teachers, but their brand is not mine. My own classroom is usually a rather informal (some principals would call it "loose") affair with a tendency toward open discursive rambling along a full spectrum ranging from genius to sheer nonsense. Therefore, I have settled here for an informal essay treatment as the vehicle for my comment on social studies instruction. I have avoided the treatise and I congratulate myself on having done so.

Too, I believe the generalization to be among the teacher's most effective teaching weapons and I have not excluded it from this essay. Generalizations, both supportable and insupportable, and prejudices abound. They are yours for your serious consideration or not as you like. What follows, like what has thus far preceded, is a disavowal of the pseudo-scientific. There is only one footnote in the whole thing.

I apologize for none of this, having made a sincere attempt to comment intelligently upon the corporeal substance of the teaching of social studies without working any great injustice upon its vastly more important soul.

# TWO

## OUR UNFORTUNATE SATISFACTION WITH CLIO

*The dogmas of the quiet past are*
*inadequate to the stormy present.*
*Let us disenthrall ourselves.*
        *Abraham Lincoln*

Regicide is always intriguing and usually the result of desperation. The situation of the social studies programs in the public schools is desperate. The base of the so-called social studies program is history, queen of the social sciences. The fact that we are almost exclusively teaching history is undeniable. History, however, is *not* a subject area of and by itself, and yet we persist in teaching it as if it were. We have invested the study of history, at least by implication, with powers of illumination which it does not, in fact, possess. We employ the quotations and axioms of buffoons and scoundrels of the past as magical incantations to rid us of the demons which confront us in the modern world. Clio rules over all and our treatment of her amounts to pure ritualism.

The history dialogue in our classroom is innocent of meaning or relevance. It has become a seemingly endless nightmare, full of sound and fury, signifying nothing. It proceeds familiarly: "What was the year of the battle of Hastings, and identify the two principal contestants. . . . Doug? And Doug responds automatically from the depths of his mechanical training, "The date of the battle of Hastings was 1066, (though he's tempted

25

to try out 1947 just for a different effect) and the two principal contestants were William the Conqueror and King Harold of England." And so proceeds the catechism of the damned.

And in the time consumed in this innocent exchange, for which we might allow two minutes—permitting the pregnant pause while Doug rouses from his systematically induced torpor —somewhere in this world of ours a human being dies of starvation. The teacher, meanwhile, moves on to the Domesday Book. Doug goes back to sleep, a job well done. This is a horror; this is grotesque; this is insane. This is the perimeter of our investigation of man. This is our "social studies" class in action. In many instances the students involved in such labors have intellectual quotients that are multiples of that of both the textbook author and the drill instructor. The lessons lack purpose and meaning. Tolstoi once defined history as ". . . deaf men answering questions that have not been put to them." Such irrelevancies form the sum and substance of our social studies instruction.

Recently, an associate of mine in the Department of History remarked on the future of history in the classroom. His view was that Clio was not only dying, but that she was being done in systematically by something less than inspired instructors. My own experience both as an undergraduate and a graduate student of history bears the professor out. So, I suspect, does yours. As a solution he proposed the rejuvenation or, if need be, the resurrection of history. He also admitted that he did not know how to revive Clio. Yet, given this very accurate diagnosis, a careful consideration of alternatives is in order. My own feeling is that Clio's case is terminal.

Rather than make the attempt to revitalize her, I would suggest that she has lived out her normal life. The time has come to bring Clio to as swift and merciful an end as possible in the classroom, draw the curtain, toll the bell, give her a burial that befits a queen, and be done with it. And when she is dead it will be truthfully said of her that in the end she was quite senile, possessed of a vivid memory as so often attends senility, but pathetically mindless, memory without mind. She only murmured and babbled on aimlessly. As though this were not enough to justify Clio's deposition as oracle of the future, there is, further than this mindlessness, something in the old lady that is unspeakably evil and anachronistic.

History as it is presented in the classroom, by and large, high school or university, is a purely *formative* discipline. Students remember and recall, regurgitate and recite. Mentally the student remains uninvolved. The invention of the printing press should have spelled the end for such pursuits. "Every line of history," writes Benedetto Croce, "must ask a question." Rarely is history presented in such terms. History is not treated as an inquiry; it is treated as *fait accompli*. Such a thing it is not. We advance history as a body of information not necessarily related to anything enclosed by the covers of a textbook. It is taught as though it were possessed of some magic of and by itself. It is not. We wait upon history as upon the Oracle of Delphi; but we pose no questions, satisfying ourselves with the incoherent bubblings and expecting that our students will be duly impressed with the grandeur of it all. They are not, and we know better. The courses that we offer under the name of "social studies" instruction are perhaps appropriate only to professional historians and antique dealers which very few of us become. Because so much has been made of Clio, it is time to evaluate the unchallenged position that she holds at the center of social studies instruction in the schools.

While history does provide a dimension for social science investigation, it is not itself a social science (though the debate rages among academicians) by definition of terms. The formal object of the social science is the nature of man in society. Now history does provide evidence through which the nature of man may be further studied and understood, but the formal object of the historian is not human nature, but *change,* change of any description. It is the function of the historian to record and explain change. Change is a very inclusive term that obviously encompasses far more than just social change. We have histories of music, histories of the novel, histories of rock formations; There is a historical dimension to anything that changes. It is intrinsic to any process, any development. There is nothing about history, on the other hand, that is intrinsically or peculiarly "social," or necessarily related to man at all. Since man develops, of course, he, *too,* has a history. Thus history is properly seen to be an aspect of study, not somehow a separate subject area of and by itself. And we mistakenly persist in treating it as if it were just that.

When the focus of the history is man, Clio has even less pretense to being scientific, although historians do lay claim to a most elaborate epistemological system, the vaunted historical "method." The discovery of the existence of the historical method is a comparatively recent development in the evolution of historical intelligence, though historians are wont to accuse Herodotus of having applied it conscientiously. Herodotus, they say, was "scientific" because he asked questions. He also interviewed people who were contemporaries of the events which he recounts. These people, it was later discovered, were "primary sources," and primary sources have a sacrosanctity all their own for the historian. They provide lies directly, and Herodotus took them down eagerly and no doubt expanded on them for the creation of his narrative. Certainly that narrative on the Persian Wars is sufficient evidence for dismissing the charges against Herodotus that he was scientific and "the father of history."

If science is loosely defined as "systematically arranged information," then human history would meet the requirements; so, too, would the telephone directory. If we further specify that science insists upon the arrangement's being predicated upon a cause and effect relationship, it would appear at first glance that history would still qualify. But does it? We have long assumed causal connections between historical developments. But with the same academic assurance with which we accept the principle of causation (which is fundamental to the explanation of change), we may reject it. When we assert that slavery was a cause of the American Civil War, we disallow the fact that cause and effect must occur simultaneously, since slavery, we are told, existed in America since 1620 and the Civil War broke out more than two centuries later. This forces us into the exciting position of holding that for more than two hundred years a cause was existent that had no effect. A cause that has no effect is not, in fact, a *cause*. The nature of "cause" includes the notion of effect. Neither exists independently of the other. Properly understood, the two ideas do not admit the possibility of time lapse; even for the fraction of a second. A cause existing without an effect is impossible. As horridly academic as it is, the fact remains that the validity of history's most basic assumption—the principle of causation—cannot be demonstrated.

The historian escapes the philosophical net by virtue of his hindsight. He *begins* with the effect and goes on to assert the cause. If, for example, the Soviet Union were to launch a nuclear attack upon the United States tomorrow, the historian would go back into the past—perhaps to the crisis that resulted in the Berlin airlift in 1948—and establish an interlocking network of cause and effect inevitability demonstrating the systematic increase of tension between the two powers. From this vantage point the attack would be clearly understood: simple "cause and effect." But in all probability tomorrow will come and go without an attack. Then what of this beautiful logical chain of causations so readily understood? Can the historian with his scientific method begin with the present and illuminate a single step of the future with the same mystifyingly clear logic?

History then is neither necessarily social nor scientific, yet it forms the basis of the social studies curriculum as queen of the social sciences. Every historian as well as every serious student of history must, therefore, confront three questions: first, is there such a thing as historical truth? second, assuming that there is such a thing as historical "truth," can man find it? third, assuming that there is a historical "truth," and that man can find it, do we *want* it? Most historians would hesitate at the first question. Was slavery in fact a cause of the American Civil War? Was the enactment of the Fugitive Slave Law a cause of the American Civil War? Did Germany precipitate World War I? The historian balks at these and pleads qualifications; the student recites.

The question of man's objectivity in pursuing the "truth" has been treated often enough. From the German we have one view of the origins of World War I; from the Frenchman we have another. The opinions of scholars on any historical phenomenon contradict one another with such regularity that the only thing of which we can be sure is the fact that they contradict. Still the student recites. If he is alert enough to have identified the position of his text and of his instructor, he recites without mistake.

Do we *want* historical truth? Do we alter our course in the knowledge that every arms race, according to the lesson of history, has resulted in war? Do we tell our students in American History classes that Osceola was arrested under a flag of truce and hanged? History has little pretense to either truth or objectivity, which is really not so shocking because few of us take it seriously anyway. But the students *do* recite—American students, Chinese students, German students and African students—all recite.

Where there does exist the pretense of investigation in history classrooms, the subjects most often are hopelessly academic. We involve ourselves in bursts of sophistication in the world in which scholar pits himself against scholar on the question of whether or not the Ems Dispatch was, in fact, edited, whether Pericles had a cone-shaped head as Aristophanes said he did, which of *The Federalist Papers* were written by Madison and which by Jay? Even interpretive history never rises to anything higher than history. It does *not* provide an illumination of the nature of man, nor any insights into the political, social or economic behavior of man that may be used to project the future dimensions of the world's society. The very word scholarship has begun to take on a musty, sterile smell; our best minds wrangle in an arena of idiot's delight—sepulchral and antiseptic. Is this what we wish to pass on in the name of social studies instruction?

But a knowledge of the past, it is argued, is the heritage of the "cultured gentleman." Such vagueries are the stock in trade of those who can find no other justification for what they do in the classrooms. They, too, recite. They offer clichés rather than cogent arguments in support of the teaching of "history." But Santayana's statement about those who cannot remember the past being doomed to repeat it is interpreted by the students as meaning "next year again." But how are students to be convinced of the importance of historical precedent when they live in a world that insists upon re-definition of so many of our most basic understandings? Marshall McLuhan tells us about the obsolescence of linear communication; Dr. Morton White, on the advent of a successful heart transplant, asks for a new definition of death; young people interviewed on television ask for a new definition of marriage; and even the

Catholic Church hovers on the brink of new doctrinal definitions. How then do we justify the all-importance of history,
the magic of recitation? Enough of mindlessness.

Though senility itself makes Clio unfit to maintain her grip
on our time and energies, there is the further argument of her
poisonous nature. The study of history has an unfortunate
*disintegrative* impact on mankind in that, through a study of the
unique rather than the common, it emphasizes the differences
between one man and another. History has the intolerable effect
of setting nation against nation, civilization against civilization,
and man against man.

History is written by winners for winners. In spite of this, by
some strange quirk, history seems to love the loser. We remember that Lee lost at Gettysburg but few can as readily identify
the Union general who was victorious. If asked to recall a
battle of Napoleon, we fasten immediately upon Waterloo; and
while Napoleon is vivid in our memory, Wellington is considerably less so. We recall the surrender of the German VI
Army under General von Paulus without recalling the name of
the Russian commander who bested him. But history, nevertheless, is *written* by the winners. The usual theme of any history
is how the good guys (usually against impossible odds) perse-
vered and then prevailed over the bad guys, thus re-establishing
truth, justice and the god of their own ways.

The pattern is established with the oldest recorded history.
It proceeds through the books of the Old Testament and comes
into its own with Herodotus whose history recounts in magnif-
icent colors the successful struggle of the Greeks, whose strength
lay in their earnest belief in democracy, against the forces of
tyranny from the East. Livy provides us with the account of
Roman superiority over Carthage, while Tacitus in *Germania*
gives the theme a twist by extolling the virtues of the Germans
and chastising Rome with her contrasting moral decadence; but

we know in spite of appearance, whose side Tacitus is really on all the time. Caesar's *Commentaries* is much less disguised.

The historians of the Middle Ages supply a new cast of characters but the plot is the same. In the eighteenth century, Voltaire and Edward Gibbon switch the roles, unseating the Church and providing secularism with the "good guy" billing. By the following century all wraps are off and history becomes the instrument of inflammatory nationalism. We discover that the Germans, or the French, or the English or the Americans are the chosen people for whose emergence all previous history has been the preparation. Who the good guys are depends entirely upon whether we read Treitschke, Michelet, Macaulay or George Bancroft. Other historians of the period, Fiske and Gobineau, for example, set the dichotomy in terms of racial distinctions. Others made religious distinctions. Among them was Francis Parkman, who pleaded the magnificence of Protestantism as arrayed against the puny anemia of the papacy. As we listen to Wolfe reading from Gray's *Elegy* to his troops, there can be no doubt who will be victor on the morrow. Winston Churchill's monumental six-volume account of *The Second World War* is cast as a morality play. And the reader thrills to Leonidas' stand at Thermopylae and the sinking of the *Bismarck*. We are the heirs of superiority. We are most naturally gratified with the series of rationales of success that makes up the historiography of the western world.

But meanwhile the world has become larger and larger and the good guy-bad guy theme correspondingly more and more anachronistic. The study of history, emphasizing as it does the differences between *us* and *them,* and clearly distinguishing the superior from the inferior, has an unfortunate *dis*integrating impact on mankind. It is incompatible with the mutual understanding and harmony necessary to survival in our present world. It may well be that national pride served a useful purpose at one time, but that time is gone. Where it once served the tendency of men to consolidate, it now serves to divide. The luxury of the us-them consideration is one that we can no longer afford.

Today it has become abundantly clear that any society which allows its members to be guided by such narcissistic myth-making jeopardizes more and more of its aspirations to political, economic and cultural survival. The lessons of the late 19th and early 20th centuries are forceful enough. In a day of nu-clear weaponry it is assured that not even the flower will remain to mark the place where Narcissus searched the pool enamored of his own image and perished in an ecstasy of self-importance. The chief function of the instruction we offer to students who plan to live most of their adult lives in the 21st century is to illuminate the need for macrocosmic perception, to assure that they identify themselves in grander terms—as men. Leaving idealism aside for the moment, the purely pragmatic considera-tion of survival of our own civilization and that of others demands the re-organization of the social studies curriculum along the lines that will guarantee it.

Few histories, excepting those of H. G. Wells and Will and Ariel Durant, offer the world view appropriate to our real and present needs. Such titanic works as undertake to depict the total human community must be written from the viewpoint of man. The history of a nation or a race (for example of the American people) is a decidedly more narrow focus, and must invariably root in the Us-Them principle. History then ranges on a spectrum from philosophy to gossip in proportion to the comprehensiveness of the viewpoint. The study of history as we pursue it is, in every sense of the word, lethal. Happily it is the history of H. G. Wells and the Durants that is most widely read. (They're rarely used in the classroom.)

From the pedagogical point of view, the manner in which

most teachers attempt to present history, that is, the survey, is futile. Most surveys offered in university or secondary schools are comprehensive enough to defy the average student's interest or mastery. After the examination little remains with him except a lethal inoculation of us-themism. Even the instructor who has been teaching the course for years finds that he must brush up on the details before presenting his lecture in class. He has first-hand experience of how little sinks in. Yet he persists. And each year he drags out the old notes and readies them for his new batch of unsuspecting Pinocchios. Even if the study of history did have some intrinsic value, the chronological survey approach would render it sterile.

An alternative to the survey approach is the problems approach which has been enjoying something of a resurgence in the classroom since the close of World War II. The difficulty with the in-depth study is two-fold. The first difficulty is that the historical problem, for example, "Was the Reformation a part of the European Renaissance?", will most likely be treated in a purely historical context, that is, isolated as a unique event, and thus rendered antiseptically academic. The solution of such a problem (if there is one, and if it is a problem) is more properly the lifetime project of a professional historian who has nothing better to do than the six-weeks' project of a live high school student who should have a good many more important things on his mind. Bluntly, what does he care? What sort of world would it be if he *did?*

A second difficulty with the problems approach is in no way offset by educators who argue that it is not the solution but the application of the *method* that is important. Of what value is learning the method of a study, if the subject of the study is itself irrelevant? Moreover, the historical method itself shrivels into an epistemological ballyhoo that cannot survive the first of the three questions raised above, "Is there a historical *truth?*"

Might we not learn method as well by applying it to questions that will take us somewhere?

What then is the proper role of history in the curriculum? First, lest we be accused of wanting to turn everything to use, let us consider that history courses should be offered at the secondary and university levels for the benefit of those who delight in the past. (We shall disallow the fact that their reading will further their delight much more than a series of tedious lectures.) In my own attendance of history classes (which was sporadic, indeed), I regularly found myself wondering what the function of the instructor was. History is a reading course; it lends itself readily to being *learned* but considerably less to being *taught*. In any event, the fact that a handful of students have a history hang-up is certainly no justification for requiring it of all students. But, runs the argument, if history were an elective, then most students wouldn't take it. This may hurt our pride—those of us who do love history and wish to share it with the younger generation—but the name of the game is *public* education. Some like Bach; more prefer something else. There are thousands of healthy, normal human beings who live out their lives quite happily without ever having heard of the Stuart kings.

But there is another role for history in the curriculum, its role as a dimension of social science investigation. This role, a most important one, is defined and illustrated in another chapter.

History for the sake of history is inappropriate to public education on several counts. We have considered its content here. It is dull, usually meaningless (ask the students—I'm talking about the *classroom*), and, by nature, poisonous. The method of teaching so naturally employed in presenting history is yet another horror, and it is treated elsewhere.

# THREE

## A SOCIAL STUDIES PROGRAM
## IN FACT AS WELL AS IN NAME

*The proper study of Man is Man.*
          *Alexander Pope*

At a time when our social studies programs should be of top quality, they are dismally mediocre. Instead of generating bold and intelligent response to world issues they produce only hollow echoes of Thebes and Camelot. Where we need vitality and action we find apathy and inertia. Social studies instruction in North America is social studies in name only. The result is that "social" is perhaps the most unpopular course given at the high school level or, to borrow the more apt high school colloquium, a "waste." Our secondary level course offerings in the social studies bear little resemblance to social science, and thousands of students rediscover each day that their social studies classes aren't worth attending. What we are teaching is history. Even well done this does not add up to social studies.

From time to time the conscience-stricken teacher, in an effort to invest the past with some measure of importance, makes some feeble gesture toward "relating" it to the present day. Whatever "relevance" emerges from the process is purely illusory, because the focus of attention is *still* upon explaining the *past*. In the bargain Clio is often maimed beyond recognition. The principal distinction we ourselves must make before

embarking on a program of instruction is whether our control-
ling purpose is to explain the past making use of what we know
today, or to explain the present making use of the past. The
former is purely and simply a study of history, while the latter is
the proper intent of the program in social studies. Rather than
beginning with the answer and searching for the question, genuine relevance is established by beginning with a *question*.

The relevance of what we're doing under the label of social
studies instruction is at once the most crucial consideration and
the most suspect. A survey of North American high school
students asking which of their courses had the least relevance
would produce in the majority of instances the response, "Social." (In the United States: "Cit Ed." There, even the name of
social studies was given up for a time, and is just now making
its way back.) But whatever it's called, what is in fact "history"
would capture the distinction rather handily in spite of some
hardy competition mustered by other departments with equally
defunct curricula and teaching techniques. In the interest of
protecting the *ego,* teachers might retaliate with the rationale,
"What do *they* know?" And perhaps we permit ourselves the
comforting thought that while the students don't respond positively now, there will come a time in their maturity when they
will realize the value of what we have "taught" them about
Richard III and the children in the tower. Do we really believe
this? Current curriculum and practices suggest that we do
indeed.

Regardless of how important Edward V is to the teacher,
who in all probability was a history major, the more essential
consideration is that the students don't see (whether rightly or
wrongly, and the point of this essay is that they're more sinned
against than sinners) the importance of what they're being required to "learn." Groping for relationships between the 15th
century event and the present day will not invest that event with

relevance. The intolerable burden of having to learn something that has no relevance is a species of torment that should be reserved for the deepest pit of hell. Which of us would enjoy the prospect of "learning" a page from the local telephone directory? Such things pass in many "social studies" classrooms as some sort of intellectual accomplishment. In fact, it is a form of idiot's delight. "I don't know the date of the battle of Tours," said a very eminent European historian, "and I don't care." Every schoolboy does. He *has* to care.

This is unquestionably the character of much of what passes for social studies instruction. It is propped up by a formidable network of quizzes and examinations upon which depends nothing less than the student's future. Nothing less significant could possibly compel the human mind to such absurdity as it is driven to in the classroom. The only real relevance of the things that the student is learning is that failing to do so results in forfeiting his opportunity to go on to university (where very often he is put through the same sort of mindless exercise). The new carrot is the degree, and the indenture is not finally worked off until the achievement of the coveted doctorate. The net result is the incredible disparity between our "education" and our intellectual development, between what we've been "taught" and what we *know*.

Additionally disturbing is the point that no one should be more sensible to the inanity of forced concentration upon the irrelevant than the teacher who, in pursuit of accumulated credit hours and advanced degrees, is himself victimized by uninspired instruction and irrelevant content. Yet, despite their own disenchantment and despair, these same teachers become the instruments of torture in their own classes. If the teacher is not the guardian of intellectual integrity, then who is? Who *will* bridle? Who *will* say, "Enough"?

The function of a social studies program is to introduce the student to the objectives, the methods and applications of the social sciences, and to bring him, through such a consideration, to a greater understanding of himself and of his fellow men. The task of the social scientist is to explore the nature of man in society, and through this exploration, to illuminate man's political, economic and social nature. It is his purpose to discover and identify the laws governing human behavior that account for the economic, political and cultural phenomena that we observe. It is his hope that as the laws that regulate human behavior are established, our understanding them will serve as a basis upon which to predicate a course of action in guiding man's relationship to man in order to guarantee maximum satisfaction of man's ends for the greatest number, and with the greatest hope of continuing regularity. In this social studies is essentially *informative:* beginning with the question of what man is and proceeding systematically toward understanding. A social studies curriculum for the elementary-secondary school program should be organized around carefully selected problems that demand man's attention. Such a program could be engineered and articulated in one summer by a handful of interested social studies teachers. Several topics or problems suggest themselves at once: law, revolution, communication, war, poverty, starvation, ethos, nationalism, imperialism, ideology and the specific ideologies, as well as the more controversial topics including such things as race, religion, population and its control, public and private morality, sex, marriage, and so on. Today's propensity is to avoid the controversial subjects in social studies classes precisely because they are controversial. So we settle things in the streets during the summer.

The list of topics worthy of attention is endless: fanaticism, censorship, herd instinct, charisma, loneliness. Students at any grade level cannot help but respond to a thoughtful selection of such fascinating topics for investigation, providing that the treatment of the concepts involved is appropriate to their age group, and that they are led by interested and informed instructors. An attendant feature of introducing such a program would be the necessity of generally re-appraising student "maturity." One social studies teacher remarked to me that when he asked his "slow" class what they'd like to study (the "slow" group curriculum is generally more flexible—that is to say, uncluttered), one teenager responded earnestly, "Let's talk about LSD; we're too dumb for the academic stuff."

In all events, the thing to be avoided in the re-organization of the social studies curriculum is the replacement of the history course with a course in the principles of sociology. This is simply to exchange masters. What is needed is an *integrated* social science approach that does not lead us again into the study of a discipline as a discipline for the sake of the discipline. The idea is rather to shift the social studies curriculum from its largely formative present role to an *in*formative one. It is this that seems to dictate that the curriculum be organized around specific problems and that in their investigation it draw upon all of the social sciences, upon history, philosophy, religion and others among the humanities. The key is to pull down the walls constructed and maintained by jealous academicians, and to allow ourselves to be guided by our own curiosity and interest. We shall learn things as we have need of them, and our discoveries will unfold new questions. Learning is confrontation with the unknown; it carries with it its own relevance.

It must be noted also that the shift to a social science base in the establishment of a genuine social studies curriculum would entail a large scale re-organization of teacher preparation programs in universities and of teacher certification requirements imposed by the various licensing agencies (which are not normally under teacher regulation). Leaving the compilation of figures and details to the professional "researchers," it may be estimated that the vast majority of our social studies teachers are history majors, not social scientists at all. Among them there appear to be comparatively few economics or political science majors. Courses in anthropology or sociology do not show up with any regularity in the background of social studies teachers, and those with a background in social psychology are a rarity. Geography seems to have fared somewhat better as a part of the teacher's training, but as that discipline becomes increasingly complex and demanding, this aspect of the social studies teacher's education also becomes woefully inadequate.

Revision of certification requirements is long overdue. The need for revision is widespread and the revisions must be sweeping; and even though many deeply vested interests will have to be rooted out, the process of revision need not be overly involved. Were there a professional teachers' association that regulated the qualifications of its members there would be little or no difficulty whatever. Teachers, after all, are better informed as to the academic background demanded of them by what they want to do in their classrooms than those who presently regulate such things, and who design large scale curriculum syllabi for vast geographic chunks with little regard for individual differences.

If we are to teach a social studies program, it is imperative that our teachers be provided with a broad preparation, one that will guarantee that they are grounded at least in economics, political science, sociology, anthropology, social psychology and geography as well as in history. Breadth of preparation becomes essential to the necessary expansion of our interest, and such breadth is vastly more useful in the high school classroom than a specialization in ancient history. The fact that at the moment it might not be is indicative only of how poor our curriculum is. It should also be noted that the necessary flexibility could be built into the teacher's preparation by a general clearing of the

legion education course requirements so many of which serve
no useful function whatever. Thus we would make room for the
pursuit of interest in fine arts, literature, philosophy and comparative religion, science, and mathematics, any or all of which
would enhance his teaching performance.

Our teacher preparation programs should be characterized
by breadth, flexibility, and an emphasis upon content. Certainly
there is no question whether or not this can be done—and we
do not disallow for a single moment the formidable forces of our
highly organized inertia—it simply *must* be done. Some of my
colleagues complain that "our social studies courses are given
by the gym teachers." But whose fault is this?

We seem to be calling for a social studies teacher who is
a "Renaissance Man." This is not the case exactly; there is an
important distinction to be drawn first. The Renaissance Man is
not the Renaissance Man because he is master of all surveyable
knowledge. He is a Renaissance Man not because he is omnis-
cient (which is more unthinkable in the 20th century than it
was in the 13th) but rather because of the breadth of his
*interests*. He cannot be master of all fields, but he must be
*acquainted* with many and disposed to make inquiry into any
that serve his investigation. Being a Renaissance Man is, in the
20th century, a question of temperament rather than intellectual
achievement. Such a model is worthy of the emulation of students. The teacher's function is to be able to open as many
doors as possible, not necessarily to be able to conduct tours
into the furthest reaches of the new domains. He must know
enough to be able to project to his students what might lie un-
discovered there. He must be conversant enough to fire the
imagination of his students so as to push them ahead into
places that he cannot go—for want of *time,* not of interest.

The key to successful teaching, then, is not in having all the
answers. This, in fact, is not only impossible, but a positive

hindrance. The gifted teacher applies his own learning and experience through being able to pose the right *questions*. To propose the right question is to enkindle a fire in the mind; to provide the answer is to run grave risk of extinguishing it. A mind well stocked with unanswered questions is the mark of the educated person; a mind stocked with hand-me-down answers is the mark of the dolt.

The objections to such a proposed curriculum would be the usual heart-rending pleas that characterize our all-consuming inertia: "What about Edward V?" "I haven't the *time* for such a thing." "I'm thinking about this sort of thing but Rome wasn't built in a day." "I'd like to do it but what would the parents say?" (I propose that we *ask* the parents instead of assuming their reaction and then using them as a whipping boy for our own laziness.) "I'd like to do it, but there's no one else with any imagination around here." "There aren't any sources for this kind of thing." *Nonsense!*

Formidable obstruction comes, too, from the great unifiers; those who will weep that not all the students will be learning the same thing. In the ideal society, the argument must run I suppose, everybody knows the same thing. Then of course, it's easier to test everybody, also easier to score. And on and on. But the world doesn't revolve around the coming exam, and ultimately success depends, however unfortunately, upon what we know. Nor should our learning be restricted by what we are able to measure. The only concession possible to the grinding practicality of these people is that assuredly we can produce tests imaginative enough to match—and not retard—imaginative curriculum and teaching techniques. And if the testers cannot stay up with the teachers, I guess they'll fall behind.

The development of the student's intellectual processes is served handsomely by instruction established on a truly social science base. Instead of answers that have no questions, we pursue relevant knowledge, even into the darkness. The understandings and skills that we develop are durable and have direct application, that is, they bear direct relation to our own humanity and to life itself. We do not expect that through such a program the sixteen-year-old high school graduate will have the answers to the world's problems; but through concerted attention to the development of his mental processes, he will have developed a method of thinking that will enable him to be captain of his own destiny—or at least intellectually prepared to confront it. He is much more likely to be an activist than a slug, to be a reader rather than a brawler, to hold informed opinion rather than a Molotov cocktail, to be useful to himself and others rather than a delinquent. His chief asset will be that, like his teachers, he won't have all the answers but will be pointedly aware of his unanswered questions. Rather than go into the world naked at least he is armed with the realization that there are questions.

Of even greater importance perhaps is the transformation that takes place in the affective domain by shifting to a social science base. Mr. Norman Cousins, addressing a large group of high school teachers a few years ago, remarked that he was "half educated." Said he, "I was educated to live in half a world —the white, western half." For all the modesty of the statement I was struck with what was in fact a substantial indictment of much of what I and undoubtedly others were doing. We are still doing it. As the futility of our effort grows more and more obvious, and its consequences clearer and clearer, I cannot refrain from calling the remark to the attention of other teachers. That we do not understand our fellow men is abundantly obvious. We gasp in disbelief at riots and church bombings, at news reports of lynchings and snipers. We plan bomb shelters and tune in police broadcasts that tell us how to defend our homes against our neighbors. We marvel at the vigor of the struggle of new nations prying loose their independence though there have been more than fifty since World War II. We have come to expect war in the Middle East as a part of life. We are forced to accustom ourselves to violence and insanity. We are not disposed to confront the realization that we cannot simply ignore the existence of people whose ideologies and values are different from our own. We have not been prepared intellectually to prevent, to cope, or even to anticipate. We simply do not understand.

Understanding is not simply a cognitive process; it is affective as well. In its intellectual sense it cannot be developed apart from concurrent development of the values of tolerance and compassion. The most important single thing to be promoted by any educational system is compassion; if nothing else emerges, then this at least. Compassion is both the natural result of intellectual understanding and the necessary requisite to it. The age old problem is not only that we *don't* see, but that we *won't*. Men without understanding in the full meaning of the word are useless at a conference table, and it is the conference table that has become the arena of conflicting values. Since the alternatives to negotiation are now unthinkable, we cannot afford to be represented by people who are *temperamentally* unprepared to cope with the unfamiliar. In addressing himself to the *Pueblo* crisis in January 1968, the chairman of the Armed Services Committee of the United States House of Representatives declared for the world to hear: "I don't make any pretense of trying to understand the Oriental mind." Asked if he would make use of nuclear weapons to solve the problem, the gentleman replied, "So fast it would make your head swim."

Nor can we afford the latent menace of a populace indisposed to try to understand. The days of wearing our guns low are gone and the social studies programs in our public schools must be altered accordingly. What significant large-scale re-organization of curriculum has taken place that would indicate our awareness of the new era ushered in by the explosion of the first nuclear bomb? Since 1945 the world has blundered from one crisis to another with neither method nor direction. Education is the only instrument of control. And the principal burden of producing that control falls squarely upon the social studies teacher.

The burden upon him is to promote the posture of compassion or *sympatico* through which students can anticipate change and make the modifications necessary to assure their own survival and that of their fellow men. No society or system can be allowed to remain outside our ken—particularly *not* those that stand in diametric opposition to our own. Nothing of human nature can be allowed to remain unfamiliar to us for want of the effort. No avenues of investigation into the similarities among men that might yield a possibility of greater harmony between them can be left unexplored. Accidental differences that separate men must be recognized and identified and then put aside in the effort to uncover the essential sameness of all men. History, taken in its own terms, is unequal to the task. What is required is the larger view of the social scientist. His objective drives him to an examination of what is common to men, not to the delineation of their differences. This makes his investigation more appropriate and more serviceable to the globe's future inhabitants. The differences among us soon become clear enough, but our focus should be directed to our sameness—black, white, Jew, Hindu, German or Polynesian. Anthropology has been suggested as an appropriate base for a social studies curriculum. Given our present needs, I could not concur more wholeheartedly or enthusiastically.

This is the task of the social studies program that is worthy of the name and worthy of the serious attention of teachers and students in the classroom. We must admit that they will not solve the problems, but we can be confident that they'll be *disposed* to solve them, and that disposition is the necessary first step. The devices for generating it must be carefully and deliberately built into the program of instruction without concern for our attachment to Edward V. Rather than work on the development of an appreciation of the past, let us work to develop an appreciation of the future so that we may guarantee ourselves, among other things, the opportunity to reminisce.

The social studies curriculum should not be a "waste." It could be and should be purposeful and very exciting, the most worthwhile part of the high school program.

# FOUR

## SOCIAL STUDIES CONCEPTS
## AND THE USE OF GOOD BOOKS

One of the most striking differences between the 4th period social studies class and the 5th period literature class is that the literature teacher assumes a fair amount of literacy and goes on from there to provide decent books for his students to read. Regardless of the personal attributes of the instructor, no class in American literature can be a total loss, because the instructor has Hawthorne, Melville, Twain, Hemingway and Faulkner going for him, almost in the role of guest lectures. In world literature classes in the United States students read Homer, Chaucer, Dante, Shakespeare, Dickens, Gogol and D. H. Lawrence. And in their world history classes are they reading Herodotus, Thucydides, Tacitus, Suetonius, Voltaire, Macaulay and Pirenne? Hardly. They read a textbook, or at least they're given a textbook, seven hundred and fifty pages of chloroform in print, often written by excruciatingly mediocre individuals who skim the development of mankind from then until now with neither wit nor imagination and are firmly dedicated, in collaboration with the publisher, to non-controversial pap that will capture a national market—the supreme example of the bland leading the bland. As a history major, I can honestly say that I am in full sympathy with the student who gives it up in disgust. So do I. Perhaps I am premature to conclude in this essay that history instruction has failed in the classroom and that in considering what it is that we offer as history, Clio never had a chance.

Nevertheless, for reasons developed earlier, even genuine history is not what we need. For purposes of the development of our understanding of the nature of man, a systematic study of human nature as is revealed in any of innumerable works of fiction is vastly more suitable and enlightening. Albert Camus or Henrik Ibsen can tell us much more about what we ought to know of man than Edward Gibbon. Mark Twain's *Huckleberry Finn* is a more genuinely enlightening treatment of ante-bellum America and its problems than any of the "historical" works that have appeared to date. Of course the authors of period novels must be saturated with the flavor they're re-creating. The historian writes of events from piles of notes.

The carefully chosen novel is the ideal "text" through which the social studies teacher can lead his students to an investigation of social science concepts and the discovery or formulation of the laws that govern man's economic, political and cultural behavior. The carefully selected novel provides the social studies class with the opportunity of studying a "frozen" society at whatever pace and in whatever depth the teacher and his students may find desirable. Once familiar with the application of social science method, the student is equipped to experiment with the dynamic and less controlled "real life" society. Once possessed of the ideas of what to look for and how to go about finding it, the student is ready to undertake the investigation of the people living on the Indian-Pakistani border, to observe and evaluate intelligently, and to make some prognostication respecting their future. He can become a trained observer and analyst and in the process nourishes a growing interest in people and their problems.

It is possible—even highly probable—that an average human being could force his way through the wealth of historical material on the rise and fall of the Third Reich and remain unaffected—oblivious to the human factor. Few, if any students, on the other hand, can remain unaffected by Anne Frank's *The Diary of a Young Girl*. While perhaps of less value to the professional historian, *The Diary of a Young Girl* is vastly more suited to the accomplishment of those goals implicit in the idea of public education. The novel and the study of *people* is infectious; the sad truth about the history that we present is that it possesses instead the character of an inoculation which for many students guarantees a lifetime of immunity.

The assignment that I have used in teaching the methods course is to have the student imagine that he has been charged with teaching a class of thirty students something about social studies. There are no history texts available, but several copies of William Golding's *Lord of the Flies* are at hand. From this the student is to organize a teaching unit. (I select this particular work because it can be read intelligently at the junior and senior high school levels as well as at a university level, because it is available in inexpensive paperbound edition and because, in addition to its power as a novel, it is so wonderfully structured that the systematic economic, political and cultural deterioration of a society unfolds under any careful investigation. (A list of other random suggestions of particularly useful novels is appended at the end of this chapter.)

It is imperative that we begin the construction of the teaching unit with a most careful definition of our objectives—the most important single process in the preparation of any course, unit or daily lesson. Because we assume that this is the class's *first* experiment with the mental processes involved in the social science method, we pay deliberate attention to the processes themselves in addition to what they yield. Our principal objective is the demonstration of *method*. The actual *findings* in our initial attempt are, for the moment, of secondary importance.

The class sessions which open the unit are devoted to the *collective* definition of the unit's objectives. To be sure, the teacher could save time by writing down *his* objectives on the board for the students to record in their notebooks. This will not do. The idea is not to save time but to involve the students in defining for themselves what it is they are going to be doing. This requires careful and systematic questioning by the teacher and may take more than one period.

The students have read the novel and know the story of a group of boys, stranded on an island without adult authority, who gradually lose the veneer of civilization. The teacher may wisely elect to suggest that they *not* read the concluding chapter in which the arrival of a ship and naval officer rescues the society from murderous savagery. (I suspect that the student will not be disposed to put the book down without reading the conclusion, even in the interest of science.) To draw the students into a definition of unit objectives, the teacher might open with a general discussion: Do you think such a thing could really happen to a group of human beings, or is this pure fantasy? This should present some generalizations on the nature of man. We begin with the process of generalizing; it is perhaps the most familiar to us. Having written several such generalizations on the board, the teacher poses, "What specific evidence can you cite to support any of these? Variety in the "evidence" offered by the class indicates an inequality in the powers of observation, and perhaps inference, among class members.

Then the point that *there is a facility for, or a power of, observation* should be made clear by the teacher. "Do you think that a trained detective could find even more evidence to support your *hypothesis?*—a good point at which to introduce the term: What is a hypothesis? How might you *test* or verify a hypothesis? Apart from our consideration of this particular society, are there other evidences you could cite to support any of these hypotheses? How many *distinct* mental processes can you identify in the development of an understanding of human nature? Are these same processes which you have just been through a part of the investigation of *any* human society?"

From this combination of questions the definition of the unit objectives should emerge. For my part, the affective objectives are of no concern for the moment. Note, too, that objectives relating to "information" and "understandings" cannot be stated beforehand. This is as it should be. We are beginning this study with questions—not answers. What we have for objectives are these, all relating to skills:

1. To develop the faculty of observing and of classifying observations of political, economic and social behavior;
2. To develop the faculty of increasing knowledge of human phenomena by a process of inference from observations;
3. To develop the faculty of formulating hypotheses on the basis of observation that would explain the phenomena;
4. To develop the faculty for testing the hypotheses for their reliability.

The second phase of the investigation might be used to demonstrate the need and value of some system of classification of evidence. What do we mean by *classification?* Why does science *classify* information? The value of classifying information to make it manageable can be brought out by having students identify a number of "crises" in the systematic deterioration of the boys' society. What specific incidents can you recall that illustrate the gradual breakdown of the society? Can any of these incidents (listed on the board) be grouped together? Why do we include some incidents in our grouping and exclude others? What, then, is the *basis* of our classification system? It may be necessary, in the event that only political or economic crises have been identified in the discussions, for the teacher to ask whether Jack's painting of his face was in any way a crisis? Once the distinction between kinds of activity is made, it is wise to elicit more examples of each of the three (political, economic and social) to anchor the students' understanding of the basis of this particular classification system. This phase might finish by calling attention to the requisites of a sound system of classification: that, first, it must be *comprehensive* so that any evidence uncovered can be fitted somewhere, however tenuously, and, second, that the distinction between categories must be as complete as possible. Such questions as, "Can anyone suggest any activity of man that is *not* either political, economic, or social? How would you distinguish political from economic activity? Here we conclude by eliciting definitions and examples of the three.

With the ground work of a social science investigation thus laid, the investigation proceeds with the establishment of three committees, one to examine each of our considerations: the political, economic and cultural behavior of the society at hand. We return to the normal step-by-step process of investigation and analyze each area in turn, combining independent committee work with reports followed by general class discussion of findings. There follows an outline of the direction such a venture might follow. There is no intention of prescription, nor do we intend that each consideration be confined to a single day's lesson. Rather, time for committee work and class reporting and discussion should be allotted by the teacher in accord with the demands of his own situation.

The first step of each of the three committees is that of *observation* to collect evidence of the society's behavior in the economic, political or cultural sphere. Rather than a random listing of observations, it is suggested that they begin by identifying what appeared to them to be "crucial" incidents. As the three committees report their respective lists of "crises," it is useful to point out that their selection has been based either consciously or unconsciously on predetermined hypotheses. Their selection has been conditioned by their notion or notions of "critical." These notions are based necessarily upon previous experience. In all likelihood the committee that presents the list of critical incidents has not undertaken at the outset to agree upon a definition of the term "crucial." Their agreement upon the events does, however, indicate substantial agreement on the notion. It is useful to take time out, when the lists of all three committees have been presented and recorded, to *define* "crucial." It becomes clear in the process that the definition can be worked out beforehand as the basis for selecting certain events and excluding others, that is, an *a priori* judgment; or the definition may evolve from the list by the process of abstracting the note that is common to all, that is, the *a posteriori* method. In either event the definition is likely to change when matched with the events, or the list of incidents may suffer additions or deletions when the more precise definition is established. This exercise in careful definition of terms is a valuable one and is fundamental to the process of observation and the subsequent use of observations.

The process of observation continues with a more careful analysis of the conditions from which each incident arose. Seemingly unimportant events connected with critical incidents are often discovered to be very meaningful in the new context. This discovery is indicative, of course, of a growing power of observation. This power increases with practice and the teacher wisely provides his committees with time to experiment with as many events as possible.

In the second step the committees learn to generalize or to form hypotheses or assumptions on the basis of the accumulated evidence. Hypotheses formulated by a group of my own students after an examination of developments in *Lord of The Flies* include: "Strong leaders tend to stabilize a society." "When a society resolves a conflict it tends to reorganize itself in terms of a new authority." "A stabilized hierarchy of powers is necessary to attain social goals." "Factionalism tends to yield strong authority." "Democracy tends ultimately toward totalitarianism." This last was produced, as far as I know, independently of a review of the ideas of Aristotle. Each of these represents the work of a committee studying the political behavior of the boys. The two other committees produced similarly interesting and gratifying results in their respective fields. The range between the fairly obvious and the quite sophisticated assumptions is apparent. It is important that the teacher emphasize the rules for forming valid assumptions: that the assumption be based upon sufficient evidence, that there be no outstanding body of evidence tending to impeach or contradict the assumption, and that the assumption be drawn validly from the evidence at hand without undergoing any unwarranted expansion of meaning or application. The teacher will wisely take the time to distinguish between the distinct qualities of "truth" and "validity" in assumptions, eliciting from the class examples of hypotheses that are "valid" but not "true," and "true" but not "valid." It is likewise important to demonstrate that reliability is contingent upon *both*.

Once a series of worthwhile assumptions has been established, the class is ready to turn its attention to the testing of their reliability by re-applying them in new or unfamiliar instances. The student must be directed to sources against which he validates, invalidates or modifies the original assumption. The teacher must make the students aware of the tendency to verify one's own assumptions and to refute those of others. The independent experience of other societies serves as a proving ground. The reservoir of human experience includes history, other novels, and current commentary such as that provided by news media and periodicals. Certainly the use of personal experience to corroborate assumptions is admissible but limited on two counts: first, the probability of insufficient amount and second, the absence of true verification by an *outside* source. True verification requires independent sources.

When the observations have been massed and classified, and when the assumptions yielded have been tested for reliability, there remains the exciting prospect of projecting the future of the society on the basis of our understandings. At this point it is useful to sort out which of our assumptions involve constants such as, for example, those relating to human nature, and which involve variables or conditionals such as, for example, if Piggy's specs are broken, then the lighting of the rescue fire becomes impossible. That man creates for himself a god appears to be a constant; that his god is a golden idol is a variable. With the constants and variables distinguished, a more accurate prognostication is possible. The constants obviously can be assigned much greater weight in projecting continuation, but the variables cannot be disallowed. (Some will argue indeed that the nature of man is itself a variable.) In our story the unexpected arrival on the island of adult authority in the person of a ship's officer is a variable that could not have been anticipated, but a prognostication on the future of the society was still feasible on the basis of what we had discovered. The class had projected, without consideration of the concluding chapter, that all semblance of political, economic and social order and function as we know it was on the verge of collapse.

A further projection of social science at this point is the proposal of possible solutions. "Within the stated conditions of the society, what solutions can be proposed? Which of these solutions appear to be the most feasible? Why?" More specific testing of the class understanding of the conditions and their implications can be done: "Would the existence of a working transistor radio on the island have made a difference in the society's subsequent development? Why or why not?"

Here, in the use of an intensely interesting novel, we have an ideal introduction to the method and application of the social sciences. From it we learn more about man. Such a unit could be followed by a similar treatment of another novel focussing upon more specialized considerations: problems of racial tension and urbanization in Alan Paton's *Cry, The Beloved Country,* the ideas of human fear and hope in *The Diary of a Young Girl,* or the psychology of war in Erich Remarque's *All Quiet on the Western Front.* The possibilities are limitless. The materials are readily available, inexpensive and practically guaranteed to involve students and make a profound impact.

Considering what we're doing now with history, how can we lose?

The list of novels that follows includes other works that I have assigned in the methods course. The list is a mere fragment of great works that offer the same possibilities for a penetrating exploration of human nature. It is, of course, suggestive rather than prescriptive, although I have tried to include works that focus upon some crucial problem of mankind, and works adapted to junior high school use, as well as high school and university use:

| | |
|---|---|
| Pearl Buck: | *The Good Earth* |
| Albert Camus: | *The Plague; The Stranger* |
| Lewis Carroll: | *Alice in Wonderland; Through the Looking Glass* |

| Richard Condon: | *An Infinity of Mirrors* |
| Charles Dickens: | *Hard Times; Oliver Twist; Tale of Two Cities* |
| Aldous Huxley: | *Brave New World and Brave New World Revisited* |
| James Joyce: | *Portrait of the Artist as a Young Man* |
| Herman Melville: | *Billy Budd; Typee* |
| James Michener: | *Hawaii; The Source* |
| George Orwell: | *Animal Farm; 1984* |
| Robert Ruark: | *Something of Value* |
| A. Solzhenitsyn: | *One Day in the Life of Ivan Denisovich* |
| John Steinbeck: | *The Grapes of Wrath* |
| Jonathan Swift: | *Gulliver's Travels* |

# FIVE

## THE SOCIAL STUDIES AND
## THE MINORITY GROUP

The commitment of our society to its education system approaches the pathological. In the public schools we have focused our hopes and dreams for a better world tomorrow, and we have supported these hopes with a colossal expenditure of tax dollars amounting to billions each year. Education is the answer to all ills, and to vote against a school budget is equated with betrayal of society and of the future. In response to this wildly disproportionate confidence placed in public education, the schools publish endless lists of educational objectives which guarantee nothing short of utopian harmony, social order, and financial and cultural success. The demands and the promises compete with each other, and the wildest of them gain unrestrained support. Vast funds, national and local, spill over into disuse and waste, educators profess miracles, courses proliferate, enrollments multiply, experimental programs, both crackpot and sound, abound, and politicos anticipate fabulous returns.

Only the teachers on the firing line harbor any doubts or disillusionment. Each September students arm themselves with new notebooks and resolve to make a fresh assault. By November they, too, have joined with their instructors in a more realistic appreciation of what is going on, or, more accurately, what isn't.

How natural then that in a time of social upheaval, when war continues, negotiations balk, and riots increase, that the gauntlet should be flung to the schools, and how thoroughly in character that the schools should quixotically accept the challenge. Conditioned by all of the ballyhoo, who could conceive of a more logical place to handle the problem of racial intolerance than the school? Once again public schools roll up their sleeves with the announcement that "This is my baby." Gallant. Expected.

It is not infrequent in the teaching world that questions turn up for which there are no answers. Curious that in an age in which we have matured intellectually to the point of recognizing that there are questions for which we have no answers, we should find the unanswered question to be intolerable. So it is that we respond with masterful self-assurance, discourse calculated to dazzle with footwork, glib phrases, and the pseudoscientific jargon of the educationist. With such confidence the public schools embrace the problem of reconciling the differences between the white and black Americans.

Obviously this is a *social studies* problem. Some teenagers will handle this during the fourth period, others during the sixth period; all under the unswerving guidance of the social studies teacher. He has the proper answers and will proceed accordingly. More than this, he is guided by superior revelation to which the ordinary human being has no access, and he is possessed of some basic understanding unhampered by personal biases or emotion. Finally, he knows that his students are receptive and perfectly objective, *tabulae rasae*, and that the truth, once uncovered, will bear out the proper viewpoint.

The problem is complex, but after all, reduces to an academic question. We have in America two racially distinct culture groups, one of which has grown significant enough over the course of the past hundred years to challenge the hegemony of the other for economic and political advantages. The Afro-American stubbornly clings to his own identity, asserts his difference, and his determination to maintain it. The tendency of the majority is not to accept what is different, nor to accept the notion that anything distinct from their own society can be of value in its own right. Already at a critical juncture, the complexity of the problem is compounded by the existence of dissident elements in the minority group that insist upon integration with the majority culture, whether possible or not, and of dissident elements in the majority culture that insist upon the value of distinction.

Now where upon this spectrum does the social studies teacher take his stance? The assumption of the society that confidently turns the problem over to him must be that he stands aloof from such complexities and somehow points the way unerringly toward the truth. But there is no reason to suspect that this is the case. Reason as well as evidence indicates that he does not have the solution, nor will the students whom he is assumed to be leading. There is no guarantee even that their opinions will necessarily correspond with his. This may be either a tragedy or a blessing.

Before he teaches anything, the teacher must determine his own position. Adding to the intellectual complexities, which I am going to suggest are beyond resolution, is the complication of the ever-present ethical considerations. Is the teacher the agent of the local community that hires him and pays his salary, pledged thereby to the service of its viewpoint; or does he have a paramount responsibility to the human community, or to the academic community, which he may see himself to represent, to project his own interpretation of human values? Often he discovers a conflict in the ideals, and that conflict is brought vividly into focus by the pressure of interest groups and unrelenting individual crusaders.

But let us consider his personal view. What posture shall the white or the black teacher adopt in the public school? Theoretically, can there be a difference? Realistically, can they be the same? Which community do I represent? Is it possible that I can represent the minority interest without disrupting the majority's expectations? Shall I celebrate that which distinguishes the Afro-American from his fellow Americans, and hope that somehow by so doing I am not, in fact, driving a wedge between the two? Shall I encourage the Afro-American or even permit him to disregard that which distinguishes him from Americans with differing cultural traditions, with the notion that somehow I am helping him to a somehow greater identity? I would hesitate to adopt either tack; both are perilous.

In the academic sphere there are answers, or at least some conclusions can be reached, but how much application they have on the actual firing line is another thing. For my own part, it would seem to me that no society can be built of men who do not first respect themselves, who do not first recognize what it is that makes them distinctive and then rejoice in the distinction. One possibility, then, that offers itself is to begin by recognizing that it is cooperation, and not de-culturization through amelioration, that is the social aim we are seeking; that the very idea of cooperation assumes the existence of differences, whether reconcilable or irreconcilable, among people. The instruction would then advance along the line that carefully distinguishes between a man's identity and a man's allegiance, between the essential composite makeup of the man himself, and his accidental association, which he elects as a matter of convenience, with this or that politico-economic construct. The two are not mutually exclusive realities, but quite natural to one another. My own teaching in a high school social studies class, regardless of what particular form it took, would have to proceed from this assessment. I would expect that there are others to whom such an assessment is unacceptable. It any event, it begs more basic questions: Is this the correct guideline to civil harmony? Indeed, is civil harmony the greatest good, or even the proper province of the social studies teacher?

Have the people who are plotting the course of social studies instruction in our public schools already solved all of these problems, which is a different question from whether or not the classroom teacher has? Have we all thrown in for integration now? *And are we all agreed on exactly what that word means?* Are Afro-Americans being instructed that their values are appreciated in terms of what they *are,* rather than in terms of how closely they approximate those of the rest? Have the innocent and best-of-intentioned teachers stopped saying of other people, "So you see, class, they're really exactly like us?" As the distinctions between white and black Americans are being made clearer and clearer to each side, and as on each side the impression that the existence of the one culture poses the threat of annihilation for the other gains more and more currency, and as the Afro-American wants to know why he's studying the white man's culture, what sort of textbook are we using? Are we using a text in American history classes that offers deliberate attention to the Afro-American "contribution?" Were I an Afro-American my own response to this would be "Thanks, but no thanks." Nor would I think kindly of my new and improved American history textbook so designed that ten per cent (corresponding roughly to the percentage of the population constituted by Afro-Americans) reflected my "contribution"; so that on every tenth page I might expect to find a picture of—or at least a reference to—one of "our guys." Perhaps when my fury subsided I could summon enough charity to appreciate the gesture. I doubt it.

It is clear in such circumstances that the majority is interested in appreciating the part of me that's like them. Frankly, I'm more interested in the part of me that isn't.

All of this assumes, of course, that the classroom teacher is going to allow himself to become involved with the volatile racial question, rather than to exercise all his dexterity in skirting the issue and holding on to his job. But with Afro-Americanism commanding attention in the instructional materials, the teacher who would avoid it must become marvelously agile. There are few spots on the globe today where neutrality is a feasible alternative.

But once the individual teacher has established his position; that is, established what it is that he's going to do, is he sure that he can do it? For the moment let us take up our traditional position firmly in the middle, teaching that both man's similarities and his differences are just wonderful, that we must appreciate them both—equally if possible—and that our job is to eradicate the traces of negativism that may crop up in the discussion of how we're alike and how we're different. The problem is that if I am black and I identify myself as black, that's positive (so long as I am not black-as-opposed-to white); but if I'm black and *you* identify me as black, that's negative. Underneath all this the teacher sees his enemies to be intolerance and prejudice. So he sallies forth into battle for truth, justice and The American Way, without being altogether clear on whether discrimination is a virtue or a vice. But no matter, his targets stand out clearly enough. Here they are, outlined brilliantly against the darkness, constituting the major challenge for our public education system.

Unfortunately, and now begins consideration of the real problem, this challenge is more than a match for anything that the best of us (under the present definition of education) have to throw up against it. What are we going to do about rooting out racial intolerance and group hatred? We are going to do all that we can do, and that is practically nothing at all.

A friend of mine teaching in a small town in upstate New York told the story of how he undertook the uplifting of an honors class in high school social studies. He went after prejudice; he explained its derivation, demonstrated its want of a base in rational processes, and had the students provide examples of current non-think from their own experience. The whole thing was laid bare so that all could see—exposed. He next undertook a unit that related to Afro-American culture. He emphasized what is called today "process"; that is, he focused attention upon the processes of thought, the method of thinking. The students responded beautifully. They defined terms sharply and insisted upon definitions from others. They sorted out their judgments and re-examined the basis of each, rejecting what was unsupportable. They became accustomed to detecting fallacious reasoning, circular thinking, *non sequiturs, ad hominems,* and equivocations, and these too were laid bare to ridicule. Not even the most respected journalists, columnists and analysts escaped the glare. In short, the experiment was hugely gratifying.

One morning the normal pre-class hum was a bit louder and more agitated. A new family had moved into the community from a city ghetto. "All right, let's examine this," suggested the teacher. But there was to be no examination, no cool scientific method, no calm deliberations and conclusions. He watched in disbelief as six weeks of "education," six weeks of human progress, dropped away in great glops like a poorly done plastering job. It hadn't been poorly done; it had been thorough, carefully prepared and presented. The students had done the work themselves. But, though well done, it had been a plastering job.

Are we not asking more of our education system than it has to give? Is our confidence in the powers of education being strained to include achievements that we secretly realize cannot be reached? Are we deluding, or perhaps opiating ourselves in multiplying expenditures, providing textbooks that we hope are appropriate gestures, raising teacher salaries, providing new and better materials, guest speakers, and promoting research and field work? Hasn't every possible innovation in social studies programs and methods been tried, written up in national magazines, duplicated, and re-duplicated? Surely our basic weaknesses as people cannot stand in the face of such a financial onslaught, such a public relations job. And yet, it seems that we do still hate each other.

What then is the answer? Are we sure, to ask the more basic question, that there *is* an answer? I have none. But I do have a suspicion, a suspicion that I would suggest here only with the greatest trepidation because of my own abysmal ignorance of the arena into which I see we are being thrust. Isn't it true that basically the assumption upon which the public education system has based its attack on prejudice is that it must be combatted on *rational* ground, that the problem is rooted primarily in the cognitive domain? Whether or not we have ever made the assumption explicit, such is the ground we have chosen for our fight.

Yet we have ample evidence that suggests that this is not true; so much that few of us, if any, are under the illusion that the wise man is the good man. I have seen Ph.Ds abandoned in paroxysms of irrationality. Some of the most narrow-minded bigots we know are numbered among the most "well educated"; and, conversely, we often find people of seemingly limitless perspective among those with little or no formal education. In spite of such things, we have grappled with prejudice as some sort of intellectual deficiency to be corrected by supplying the appropriate understandings in school.

But suppose it isn't. Suppose prejudice were rooted in something much deeper than ignorance. Suppose it were rooted in fear. Suppose prejudice were essentially a psychological condition, rather than an intellectual fault. Suppose that man were driven to maintaining an opinion that he *knew* to be unsupportable or irrational, because in so doing he protected something much dearer to himself—a very tender or vulnerable psyche.

Before going any further, I should confess my own ignorance of the field of psychology. In the course of my own graduate work I took as few courses in "Ed Psych" as possible, and the ones that I did take were terrible. I can't for the life of me conceive how such a field could possibly be made dull, but "Ed Psych" professors across the country are apparently working miracles. In any event, a note of caution: as Plato put it, "What I say may not be true, but something very like it is."

To me, after ten years of teaching social studies, it seems that the notion that prejudice is rooted in ignorance is simplistic and stupid. Perhaps the great popularity of the axiom is in large part responsible for the conspicuously insignificant headway that we've made in the area. If it is already obvious to the rest of the world that our enemy lies in one frequency, and our approach in another, then why are we still stockpiling the obsolete weapons for attacking it? Where are the innovations that should have emerged in the wake of our new appraisal of the nature of prejudice, of our new recognition that we are dealing with a problem of attitudes and values rather than one of insufficient information about each other? Why do we still talk about teaching "process" as the hope of eradicating intolerance, when we have seen that human beings come to school on their very first day with an already well-developed set of values, that their schooling then takes the form of bolstering preconceived attitudes with good reasons; when we know that human beings normally tend to believe the first book that they read, and to pronounce "wrong" any subsequent opinions that disagree? A convinced Nazi who reads the New Testament does not emerge a Christian; he emerges a convinced Nazi now armed with scriptural texts. Ignorant opinion, like enlightened opinion, feeds and grows upon more information, making only the adaptations necessary to incorporate it into the system.

There is no denying that attitudes and values are moulded in the classroom, but I would suggest that, as we have seen in the case of our determined young social studies teacher above, long-term results against intolerance in a given society demand something quite beyond the most conscientious assault in the cognitive area. Contrast with his effort, for example, the more imaginative assault on the students' *psyches* directed by the elementary school teacher who divided her class into two groups for a day, separating the blue-eyed children from the brown-eyed. For the entire day the children with brown eyes were treated as a thing apart. They had to use the water fountain at the far end of the hall, and the bathroom on the next floor. Their hands were not recognized in class, and their comments ignored. Dropping a pencil or book was apt to bring the reprisal, "What do you expect from someone with brown eyes?" The next day, the teacher reversed the roles and the blue-eyes learned what it was to be "inferior." She used two days. He had used six weeks. She (perhaps instinctively—as good teachers so often act) knew her target. Her "lesson" will last each child about one lifetime; his vanished overnight. In the cognitive realm, such successes as do appear are fleeting, unstable and small-scale. We have a problem that is continuing and full scale.

The inculcation or transplanting of values is a very subtle procedure and forces us into speculation on an entirely new dimension of education. I say "new" though our great long lists of teaching objectives have included aims relating to attitudes and values for a long, long time; but who has given the matter serious, systematic attention. The normal practice—even for the teacher who includes such considerations in his lesson plans— is to more or less assume that aims will be realized automatically. But, if we would pursue it seriously, and the intent of this essay is that in order to make any genuine progress in the area of intolerance we have no choice, then such a move must be both designed and implemented by professionals who are expert in their field.

Man has ventured into the area before. Every society builds values with something more than random happenstance, never altogether ineffectively, and on a large-scale basis. Mobilization of mass values and attitudes has taken place in times of crisis, and accomplished often with only the flimsiest artificial stimulation. Every education system is to some extent propagandist; and no education system, in this regard, misses its target. In a matter of months, and with a little concentrated effort, Paul Goebbels converted a nation into a grotesque with sufficient intensity to sustain it until its physical power to make war was obliterated. Examples of what has happened from time to time in the area of re-direction of mass values and attitudes, guided by systems of widely different degrees of sophistication, suggest limitless, inadequately explored possibilities.

The point that cannot be missed in each instance, however, is that mass inculcation or development of a particular value or set of values is seen to have been primarily an *emotional,* and only secondarily an intellectual, process. It is not necessary, nor even important, that man *understand* anything here. Often the beliefs that play the greatest role in shaping our actions, and to which we cling most tenaciously, are not things that are completely or even remotely understood. If we speak of adopting an attitude as "learning," then it would seem that what a man "learns" or does not "learn" is conditioned not so much by his IQ or his socio-economic background (both of which may be peripherally related), but rather by his often subconscious psychological needs. Every modern advertiser knows this. Doctor Goebbels knew it, at least intuitively. His success indicates that the psychological state of fear is perhaps the most accessible and the most satisfactory base for new "learning." We can readily see that any "learning" based upon what is so deeply a part of the nature of man, as attitudes and values are, is vastly more durable than our understandings and, in the event of a confrontation, may easily defeat an appeal to reason.

Is it odd to suppose, then, that in order to develop in men the values of mutual respect, tolerance and compassion, we might reverse the Goebbels process of learning based upon fear, and anchor the desired learning in man's peculiar sense of euphoria (whatever and wherever it is) that shows itself in such things as the "Christmas spirit?" I'm no psychologist, but I do know that there is this peculiar sense of well-being or of security, that lurks inside somewhere. Can we not find out what it is, cultivate it, and then build new learning upon it? Is it not futile to attempt to instill or develop such values in people who are afraid? Regardless of IQ or of other cognitive considerations, a man who is afraid cannot be brought to respect or value what is different from himself.

A man is not a bigot because he has a low IQ. He is not a bigot because he hasn't enough information, or because he lacks understandings that should be supplied in a social studies classroom. He isn't a bigot because he comes from an underprivileged neighborhood, or an overprivileged one. He is a bigot because he is *afraid*. When and if our education process turns and confronts that idea head-on, with all of its implications, then and only then will we begin to make headway against intolerance of what is different from ourselves. Until such time the problem remains out of our reach, and certainly beyond the reach of the social studies teacher. And were we to decide tomorrow to devote half of the high school social studies curriculum to the study of Black history and Black culture, we could sit back and rest our consciences for another ten years; but we would not have scratched the surface of the problem.

# SIX

## MOTIVATION: THE KEY TO THE WHOLE BUSINESS

The question of motivation involves one thing: the disposition, or the will, to learn. From the viewpoint of the teacher motivating is the process of moving the student's will to learn. A student is motivated when he is disposed to learn; nothing more. It is essential to a proper understanding of motivation that we distinguish between the disposition to learn, and actual learning. While hovering about the essential nature of motivation, there are several useful points to be established.

First, it seems probable that the teacher cannot create in his student a will to learn. He can create in his student a will to go through a process which has the trappings of learning—this he does by exploiting the student's will to do well on an exam, but the teacher does not create the will to learn. The reason is that it isn't necessary. There is probably no human being of normal awareness on the face of this earth who does not possess a will to learn, regardless of how undeveloped it may be. The process of teaching should be the process of expanding the student's will to learn, of conditioning it to respond to a variety of stimuli, to broaden and to intensify a preexistent will to learn. The success or failure of the attempt is the measure of effective

*73*

or ineffective teaching—or, more accurately, of teaching or non-teaching. Implicit in this distinction is the necessary differentiation between teaching and training.

A second useful point is that a genuine motivation is the prerequisite of true learning. Motivation does not include the idea of learning any more than the will to do something is synonymous with *doing* it. Thus guidance counselors are fond of identifying "underachievers," students who have a demonstrable capacity to learn but lack either the industry *or sufficient will to learn.* "Overachievers," on the other hand, supposedly are operating at a higher level than their demonstrated capacity on the basis of sheer will—probably because at last they have encountered an effective teacher. The case of the "overachiever" is somewhat mystifying, to say the least, and reflects our inadequate understanding of the importance of the disposition to learn. I cite the cases only to clarify the essential distinction between learning and the will to learn.

The third point is that while motivation is not synonymous with learning, it is synonymous with education. Education is not synonymous with learning. Education, like motivation, is the disposition to learn. It is what remains when our learning is done. Several of my acquaintances are educated people though they could not be characterized as learned. Conversely, several very learned men of my acquaintance are not educated. It is misleading to speak of well-educated or poorly-educated people because what we really mean is well "learned" or poorly "learned." Once disposed to learn, a man cannot be systematically un-educated; a learned man can become un-learned either by "re-learning" him along different lines, or by simple disuse. Education is motivation and motivation, education.

Our inadequate grasp of the importance of the *disposition to learn* is the tragic flaw in our educational system. The results are startling. Vast numbers of students have no interest in the majority of courses they are taking. The curriculum has been imposed upon them without regard for their interests. Their learning becomes a four-year chore; and many graduate without having been educated, that is, without having been moved to an appreciation of the value of what they were doing. For them, education is a process that terminates at the age of seventeen with the vow, "I'll never read another book."

The problem here, like the problem at the college level, is a problem of motivation; it is *not* a problem of inadequate intellectual resources in either instructors or students. Yet we assume automatically when there appears to be some disenchantment with a high school or college course, that there is an intellectual difficulty; either an ineffective instructor, or a student who just can't get the material, or both. I insist that this is hopelessly naive, and that the answer to widespread disinterest in courses on our campuses is too obvious even for professional educators.

It's not the intellect that's being overtaxed; it's the *will*. Courses don't fail for want of candlepower; they fail for want of sheer stamina. Our university and high school courses aren't too tough; they're simply too long! In ninety-nine per cent of the courses given at the high school and college level, the instruction rigamarole goes on and on long after the will to learn has disappeared—months after. This is all wasted time, and such effort as there might be on the part of students or instructor is wasted, too. Probably somewhere in the neighborhood of eighty per cent of a four-year high school or college program is a waste of time, money and energy. Why does this go on? Because we have blithely ignored the *paramount* importance to the education process of the will to learn factor. From the opening of any course the student's disposition to learn diminishes constantly with each passing week; even perhaps at a fixed ratio as the depletion of carbon in organic matter, or the power of a battery at cold temperatures.

To illustrate the point let us consider the case of a bright and enthusiastic young man who, after all his degrees were accumulated and his position established, undertook a course in Shakespeare for the sheer enjoyment of it. The professor of the course was a crackerjack teacher; the content of the course compelling. Every factor promised a thoroughly useful and enjoyable experience. But the course was a full year course, two semesters, eight months, twenty-six weeks, seventy-eight class meetings, eighteen plays. What did happen was the opposite to the heartfelt intention of both instructor and student. At the end of only eight weeks the young man swore an oath that, once finished, he would never read another Shakespearean play. Multiplied by thousands of students taking hundreds of thousands of courses, this is the final impact of our educational system. The problem, put in simplest terms, is that our whole education program is designed as if for long distance runners, when the vast number of the world's students are sprinters.

From the point of view of motivation, or this question of the disposition to learn, the course should end not when the student is exhausted and disinterested or even hostile; the course should end just as the student is hitting his full stride. If the function of a course is construed to be the whetting of an appetite rather than the glutting of the appetite, it seems to me that the educational program should take the form of a mosaic. Instead of the standard semester or double semester, or even trimester course, all offerings in the humanities area should be restricted to one, two, or three-weeks. Instead of taking one course for twenty-six weeks, the student takes as many as a dozen concentrated appetizers. As there is room for six full year courses in the standard high school and college programs, the student would have the opportunity to take fifty or sixty of these mosaic pieces, each taught by an instructor who was both knowledgeable and enthusiastic. Rather than the present conception of an education as a student's beginning at one end of a two hundred-foot piece of licorice and chewing through to the other, the new conception suggests something more along the lines of the familiar sampler collection of chocolates.

The student might elect, for example, in one time slot, a two-week course in the music of J. S. Bach, a three-week course contrasting Shakespeare's *Richard* II and *Richard* III as Marlovian heroes, a one-week course in Camus' *The Stranger,* a two-week course on Michelangelo's David, and a three-week course on the fall of the Roman Empire. Thus he disposes of one of six one-hour time slots in a given semester and perhaps has found a week or two between his selections in which he can follow up an interest or take a rest.

The advantages of such an approach to liberal education would be enormous. Professors or teachers would be re-inspired finding that they no longer needed to carry out the exhausting process of padding their courses to make them stretch a full term, finding instead that they had to cull the very best they had to present on a subject, and then present it in a half-dozen sessions. Students would be invigorated, and would be meeting maximum instructor out-put with maximum student in-take; that is, they would maintain a functional level of receptivity. One year of application in such a program would seem to me the equivalent of four of the current design. The idea is in no immediate danger, of course, of undergoing any sweeping adoption, in spite of its obvious merits, because we have always with us our uncanny preoccupation with unity; and the intense little principals and deans who would be terrified that the student had no "major." But the idea does serve to illustrate the importance to the whole educational process of the disposition to learn, and the kind of exciting programming that lies within reach when we get around to giving this concern its due attention.

The appalling number of dropouts attests to the fact that we have a schooling system that emphasizes learning without education. Millions of dollars have been spent, elaborate publicity campaigns conducted urging students to stay in school, countless hours devoted by parents, teachers, principals and counselors, but nothing emerges that will answer the students' question, "What for?" The answers that are provided are hollow exhortations on the value of learning, but somewhere along the line we have missed the chance to educate. And what has been done to re-vamp the academic curriculum, to tailor it to the needs of students? The only way to keep people in school is to make school worth their time. I would suggest further that *most* of those who go on to a "higher education" do not do so because their thirst for finding out has been awakened. Ask them? "Get a better job." "Dad says it's this or the navy." "Charlie's going."

The teaching techniques employed in high school and college are molded to the all important curriculum. They are designed to get students ready for the exam, not life. The most thoughtful teacher is pressed to defend his adopted syllabus as the class asks, "What do we have to do this for?" How long can we answer the public no longer confident in the magic of what they're learning by telling them that there's going to be an exam? Yet instruction continues to revolve around mastering information, the formula for taking the volume of a cylinder, the year of the Spanish Armada, the conjugation of the verb, "être." The employed emphasis remains upon recall and recitation, but *who's selling* geometry, world history and modern language? If what we're doing is so important, where are the students who are beating down the doors of their tax-supported schools?

A third startling effect of our lack of concern for, and/or understanding of, the importance of disposition to learn is our persistence in grouping students on the basis of I.Q. Here's where the "overachiever" and his kinsman the "underachiever" continually turn up to haunt us. Such a system of grouping or "tracking" takes only incidental account of the fact of varying interests among students. Students with I.Q.'s of 130 are put into "honors" sections of each course they take on the serious misapprehension that they will sparkle. One student of mine in an American History honors class almost flunked because he was so enthralled with designing a friction-resistant nose cone, (at which he succeeded handsomely), that he could muster little interest for Andrew Jackson. (The truth is that he did flunk but was awarded a passing grade because I was interested in his interest in the problems of re-entry into the earth's atmosphere. Today he is a highly respected, highly paid engineer.) At the opposite end of the scale, the low I.Q.'s are grouped together in a caste where it is assumed that they have no interest in anything. They oblige by showing none, until they get out. Then they vote "No" on the school budget proposal. So would I. Incentive is ignored. Galileo, in all probability, would be a dropout of one of today's schools. Our society may be losing one hundred Galileos per day. Some day, hopefully, we will group according to motivation. Vocational and commercial schools will show the way to their benighted academic sister.

For the classroom teacher, motivation is the process of getting the students interested in the subject matter, at least interested enough to "learn" it. There seems to be general agreement among teachers as to the function of motivation, that it serves as some kind of emulsifying agent for mixing students and learning; but the emulsion is conceived on a grander scale by some teachers than by others. The brand of instruction that goes on in the college classroom reflects a general lack of concern for the student's disposition to learn. There the magic of the subject matter receives its fullest endorsement; and the professor either blithely assumes that the student is interested, or more cynically and correctly assumes that the student is not interested, and views his own deathless presentation as casting pearls before swine. The professor is convinced that the assassination of Philip was the most important thing that ever happened and expects that this obvious point will occur at once to any similarly intelligent human being within earshot. The most practical among them may recognize that much of this seed will fall among tares or upon rock, but in any event, there is rarely demonstrated any concern for cultivating the soil. The assumption that "they're here to learn" is demonstrably unsafe, and has been so for a long time, particularly in a day when "everybody goes to college." Professing, Abelard fashion, is not enough; what is needed is teaching. Nor do we intend a blanket condemnation, but simply to cite an example familiar to most of us. It must be readily admitted that among "professors" there are teachers. Nor has college instruction monopolized the profess-rather-than-teach approach. Many of my acquaintances among high school instructors conduct their classes as though their captive audience were graduate students, fully motivated, and with but one purpose in being there. The idea is unsafe even when applied to the majority of graduate students.

Other instructors recognize the need for cultivating student interest—for motivating—in their own subject area. Certainly this is an improvement, but it raises the old haunting question of whether we're teaching history or teaching people. Can teaching be counted a success when it has awakened an interest in one field, but not necessarily in learning in general? The teacher must indeed be gratified but also disappointed in the student's admission after class one day: "You know, I like history; you make it interesting. It's the only worthwhile course I'm taking." While we are not proposing that the history teacher is responsible for awakening the student's interest in each of his other courses chemistry, Latin and algebra, what is the source of his disappointment in the remark? Isn't he only one man doing one job and doing it apparently well?

The eminently successful history teacher does not represent the value of chemistry, or of Latin or of algebra; but he does represent more than the value of history. He represents the value of learning. This value is transmitted apart from the specific consideration of his own subject area. He is more than an interesting teacher; he is an interesting person. Once he is seen to be such by his history students, his power of projecting the value of learning, of education, becomes enormous. His influence remains long after the student's interest in the Franco-Prussian War has cooled. As the province of classroom history is expanded beyond its traditional political considerations to include the economic and cultural aspects of man, and as it yields more and more ground to the social sciences, and is coupled with other courses under the name of humanities, the teacher's power of awakening student interest in learning is multiplied by the expanded definition of the content.

Motivation cannot be assumed. It must be worked at. This is the challenge of real teaching. It is possible to distinguish two species of motivation, though the distinction becomes cloudy as the consideration is pressed. (There is ample evidence that the apparently less effective species is convertible into the more effective variety.) The distinction can be made on the basis of an evident difference in duration, one form being lasting and the other short term. The former is a genuine experience in education; the latter is not. Two often we have permitted ourselves to pretend that it is, with the disastrous result that we are now genuinely confused as to the difference. The student who has been sold the value of history on the basis of a need to pass an exam has not been *educated* regardless of his scores on the examination. The student is not appreciably different in June from what he was in September. Yet we pride ourselves on a set of high examination scores, and we are *conditioned* (the idea is unnatural) to accept test scores as the measure of the student's interest and ability. And so it is that we believe that the sort of motivation that is reflected in student's "cramming" is as good as any other. In so doing we sell ourselves, students, and learning far short. Worse, any teacher realizes this, but too often allows himself enough self-deception to get to sleep nights. I suppose most of us refuse to think about it. After all we're tackling a job of mass education and one brand of "education" becomes as good as another under these impossible circumstances. And there are these pressures, etc. However, if we're not going to *educate* the public, then let's stop wasting time and money, close the doors and learn a trade.

It is the fervent hope and implicit aim of every teacher to sell his subject in terms of its own merits, to interest each of his students on a lifetime basis. When the student's interest is in learning for its own sake, simply because he is driven by his own curiosity or fascination and enjoyment in learning, then and then only has he been educated. Education is a process involving the transformation of the *will;* intellectual transformation follows later or not at all. When the student wants to know just to know, then he's motivated. Often, it seems, this simple innocent beauty leaves them after elementary school. For the teacher the achievement of such a thing is a particularly tricky business. At the outset, it is he who makes the history fascinating. This is a challenge in itself. But once having lured the interest of his students, by virtue of his ability to make history come alive, he must carefully transfer the interest from himself to his subject so that when his students no longer have him they still have their abiding love for history. He must conceive of himself as the musician—never the music. The peculiar personality capable of both commanding the spotlight and then stepping out of it is a rare one indeed. But this is what is demanded. Irwin Edman expressed it once: the truly effective teachers were the ones we can't remember.

Probably the only ideal motivation is the appreciation of learning as an end in itself. If instruction involved sex instead of learning, the teacher's job would be a piece of cake; but the successful promotion of learning often requires treating it as a *means* to an end. While not ideal motivation in the above sense, it may be nonetheless effective. The teacher, abandoning the hope of ever motivating his students on the same basis of love that probably prompted his interest in history, is driven to advancing learning as an expedient to something else. Reasons for the learning of history range from the corny "cultured gentleman" to the romantic unreality of "good citizenship," from the utilitarian "impress your friends" to the crass "make more money" (the most effective motivator of the lot but hard to prove), from the desperate "win T.V. prizes" to the absurd and hopelessly ineffectual "there'll be a quiz on this tomorrow." This last works well enough for tomorrow, but the next day the student will be the same as he was before cracking the book—unmoved. From a practical standpoint the teacher appears to have little recourse but to the ideal. (Later chapters propose a radical solution: reorganization of the curriculum.)

But the teacher possessed of a desire to interest his students in history does have one thing going for him—a strange thing but one nevertheless to be explored. This is the curious phenomenon known, for want of a more accurate appraisal, as "pseudo-intellectualism." Successful as it may be in eluding proper definition, it is nonetheless real and widespread among human beings and particularly among students of the high school and college age. Some of the trappings by which it may often be recognized are beards, sandals, rebellious taste manifesting itself in dress and manners, or lack thereof, conversation studded with aphorisms, a distaste for romanticism and hypocrisy, devotion to obscure poets, cynicism, name dropping, and a passion for quoting the authors of books they either didn't fully understand or haven't read yet. Despite these externals, which are distasteful or distressing, such students do provide welcome relief from their more docile comrades. They are, for all, *alive*. And, more important, they are *disposed to learn*. More than this, pseudo-intellectualism is highly contagious. I suppose that a pseudo-intellectual might be defined as a person educated beyond his intelligence. The point is that they do respond to books and ideas, and they do provide teachers (particularly the more radical teachers with whom they can identify as kinsmen) with fertile ground in which to plant. They should be cultivated and, who knows, pseudo-intellectuals may grow up to be intellectuals. I'm certain that many of them do, and it might be because they ran into an inspired teacher who recognized his opportunity.

The important note is that the temporary foils that we use to motivate are of little or no value, and the horror is that they have become the basic prop under the whole works. Motivation based upon sanctions, feared or desired, does not accomplish the task of disposing the student to real learning. Motivation based upon fear is positively injurious. The birch rod is *passé;* but there are new threats of responsibility to parents and peer group, grades, quizzes and exams, college admission and an endless parade of psychological warfare which, the psychologist would probably tell us, results in a disposition *not* to learn.

Almost as lamentable is motivation based upon an endless series of carrots. When the student is carried from junior to senior high, to college, to graduate school through a Ph.D., without ever once having experienced the security of a genuine motivation, the grand prize is in many cases more closely related to a perfect attendance Sunday School pin than an index to intellectual development. Our diplomas and degrees have come to represent endurance as much as anything else. Can true education culminate in the situation in which the degree is worth more than the man is?

Realistically, the teacher genuinely transforms the will of only a comparative handful in the course of a lifetime. At that, he's a great teacher.

More specifically, what are the means of motivating students to a study of history? The most important single factor in turning the all-important trick is, as suggested above, the teacher's personality. Whatever the peculiar traits of the personality—and they vary astonishingly among the great teachers—he must himself represent the value of what he is trying to do for his students. To try to demonstrate this further is a Sisyphusian exercise of the first magnitude. There are those who undertake to calculate it all, of course, but they are not on the same frequency with the mystery they pretend to analyze. Hats off to their persistence although they will continue to be scattered in confusion.

There are three recognizable features shared by teachers who *appear* to be effectively motivating students. They can be set down and emulated because they are all tactical. First, the teacher's planning indicates that he is very much aware of his students, because the pre-requisite to any *sustained* motivation of students is *clarity*. In order for the student to become interested and stay interested, he must know exactly what his teacher is doing. When the teacher suffers a temporary loss of clarity, and the student loses the trail, he loses his interest as well, and, the chances are, will not revive it again for the remainder of the period. The effective motivator must make certain constantly that his class is with him intellectually every step of the way.

A second indication of his awareness of his audience—yes audience—is built-in drama. He deals in tension, conflict, balance, suggestion and surprise. He capitalizes on the reservoir of triumph, tragedy, pathos and magnificence, violence and misery, joy and humor, and the human interest provided in the pages of history—though often not in the textbook. People of the past are *alive* to him—never "quaint." He is familiar with them and likes or dislikes them. He avails himself of all sorts of props, and stages presentations. He insists upon his students sitting close to each other, permitting no stragglers, so that he can play to an audience and have them respond as an audience to him and to each other. *And all of this he can do very quietly without fanfare or ballyhoo.* A simple tactical move that indicates a teacher's awareness of his students is teaching with the door closed. The act of closing the door sets the stage properly.

Finally, in our consideration of some of the more basic tactics, the teacher makes wide use of *ideas*. Young people love to think big. "Facts" bore them. The human mind is thrilled with syntheses, the more all-embracing the better. Students will press the teacher for theories once they discover that he thinks. Like adults they delight in paradoxes, traps in logic, and hypotheses that fly in the face of everything that we "know." The more outlandish the idea, the more intriguing to students. Great teaching hurtles back and forth on the spectrum between genius and nonsense. This, more than any other tactic, moves the student to learn on his own. At the other end of the "think big" scale, we find that the proper presentation of minutiae also has a compelling effect. I have spent an entire class period considering and explaining the operation of the 19th century naval gun. One young man in the class became so enthralled that his interest spread to field guns and ultimately to the American Civil War. In spite of the fact that Kenny couldn't read—so said his guidance counselor—between October and June Kenny read every book in a considerable collection on the Civil War in the high school library, including Douglas Freeman's multi-volume biography of Robert E. Lee. Ken is not a historian today I'm sure, but I'll bet there isn't much time on his hands either. If he didn't mention it, I wouldn't realize today that what many would consider unjustifiable discourse on a ship's gun opened a world for a student who wasn't interested in much else.

Motivation, for all of its importance, is really very much a hit or miss proposition. If Ken had cut class again, as he was prone to do, the number of my accomplishments in ten years of teaching would be sharply reduced. And for all the discussion about motivation tactics, who knows where the spark comes from that fires the will to learn?

# SEVEN

## THE PLANNED LESSON
## AS AN ART FORM

Remarkably in an age of intense involvement in communications, there remains the great need for attention to the methods of teaching employed in our classrooms, at primary, secondary and university levels. A friend of a friend had taught history for a number of years at one of the finest liberal arts colleges in America and discovered, upon hearing a tape recording of one of his presentations, that he was a colossal bore. Blessings upon his rare soul with its curiosity to investigate and the courage to face the result without flinching. So many of my former professors I should like to invite to share the same necessary torment.

The greatest of the teachers' commandments is: "Thou shalt not bore." The fulfillment of the dictum requires but one thing: the involvement of the students. For some reason it never occurs to some teachers that it takes *two* to communicate. The narrower conception sees the teacher as some sort of towering beacon or transmitter beaming *veritas* to a roomful of thirsting receivers. It shouldn't be necessary to point out to either experienced teachers or to experienced students that the picture is not altogether correct. Somehow, however, it *is* necessary.

Human beings become involved with other human beings in two ways: intellectually and/or emotionally. Any lesson given by any teacher to any group of human beings must have the power to attract both intellectual and emotional response—usually in reverse order. The quality that attracts intellectual response is clarity. An emotional response is captured by drama. The two qualities of clarity and drama are the soul of any successful lesson; no effective lesson is without them and no lesson that contains at least some measure of each can be entirely ineffective. Some people are naturally dramatic people; others are somewhat less so. Some of us have a certain natural logic to our thinking; others do not. The point is that while some teachers can't help but be effective in the classroom, it is most often necessary that both clarity and drama be conscientiously and systematically *built* into the lesson. For some reason—one undoubtedly that our pedagogical researchers will soon have worked into an algebraic equation—the spontaneous appearance of clarity and drama comes on even better than the built-in variety. Drama, of course, has a way of spoiling when canned. Teachers find after teaching the same lesson four times that the second presentation is likely to have been better than the first—its bugs having been worked out. But the third lesson is not necessarily better than either as might be logically expected, and the fourth is decidedly less effective. The teacher by this time hears himself saying very rehearsed lines. Clarity as well as drama can be diminished as the same teacher repeats the same lesson to different students. Spontaneity, it seems, is more effective, at least to the extent that it is necessarily tailored to the immediate situation at hand.

Lessons are not pitched equally to the emotions and to the intellect. The thesis of this discussion is that all teachers should determine ahead of time whether they are pitching to a primarily intellectual target or to an emotional one. As the target varies so, too, does the method of teaching. A further thesis of this discourse is that given the two basically distinct methods of teaching—lecture and inquiry—each is more eminently suited to one target than to the other. Few teachers of my acquaintance demonstrate any sign in their teaching of having chosen their ground beforehand so as to adopt the weapons more appropriate to the circumstances. The two chapters following this undertake to identify the inquiry method with the intellect and the lecture method with the emotions. The task of the present chapter is to suggest something of the nature and value of proper planning common to both the basic approaches and any of their possible variations. The great foolhardiness of this consideration, it should be pointed out at once, is that we are examining the lesson plan, not the lesson, but the blueprint of a lesson viewed independently of that great undefinable, the teacher's personality. I am not comfortable in divorcing the two even for purposes of closer examination. An effective sketch is certainly a prerequisite to the success of a master painting, but it does not equal it.

Teaching is an art form and the lesson plan is its working sketch. As the soul of art is unity, it is unity that becomes the key to effective lesson planning. Whether the impression to be conveyed is an emotional or an intellectual one, it must be a unified impression. Any effective lecture or inquiry lesson has a totality of its own which is the result of its unity. Most beginning teachers and not a few veterans collapse in hopelessly fragmented lessons. Toward the conclusion of a lesson a teacher should be able to launch a peroration which might begin with the words: "So you see. . . ." And there should follow a conclusion or a series of conclusions made not only possible but *necessary* by the foregoing thirty minutes of work, whether done by the class or the teacher, or both. Rarely in the social studies or history classroom, at either the Ph.D. or junior high school level is such a thing possible. Far more common is the situation that ends with both bewildered students and reflective teacher asking themselves, after thirty minutes of holding forth, "So what?" Indeed many students no longer expect any unity. They have become inured to the haphazard intellectual or emotional bombardment that characterizes so much of our present day instruction and, were it not for the existence of their own random and chaotic notes, wouldn't realize they'd been to class. But for the bell system which punctuates the beginning and end of class, the instructor might go on forever. By tacit agreement students and teachers have accepted the bells as defining the development of whatever it was that they were doing. Stories are repeated of the instructors who stop mid-sentence on the bell, and who resume next class with the following word. I've known two who did just that. After twenty-five years of attending classes and ten years of watching colleagues teach, I can still count on one hand the number of teachers whose classroom presentation reflected some notion of unity. Parents have given up asking what was learned in school today. You can baffle a teacher by asking him what he taught. In either case the question is to all intents and purposes, unanswerable. Well, it should not be so.

The artist—the painter, the novelist, sculptor, poet and playwright, the composer—should be extremely attentive to and even anxious about unity. The *sonata allegro* movement, usually the first movement of the symphonies most familiar to us, is a classic model of unity to be emulated by those who prepare lessons. A lesson plan should have three distinct parts in which the theme is introduced, developed and concluded.

Lesson planning begins as the teacher is confronted by a body of subject matter, a body of "facts." Unfortunately, this is also the final stage of planning for a good many of our teachers. Their task is completed with a chopping off of this chunk at both ends in accord with what they feel can be "covered," that is, transferred to a group of students within a fixed period of time. For the history instructor there is a special windfall in that history imposes its own peculiar order on its subject— chronological order. This supplies a form of "development" which has little intrinsic relation to the pedagogical (I hate the word by this time) principle of progressing from the less to the more complex. Nevertheless, it is a species of order and enables the history teacher to rest securely, both in having "prepared" and having done so without any risk of intellectual hernia. Whether he then arrives at any meaningful conclusion depends entirely upon whether he reaches a war before the bell rings. Clio, in her infinite wisdom (and probably bored by it all anyway) punctuates her own development with wars. Otherwise, the history teacher and his kinsman, the historian, lacking in any terminal facility, pay unending tribute to continuum. Continuum is their hang-up, but the sane find it intolerable. Historical development, at any rate, is not what we mean by lesson development.

Having isolated a body of subject matter, the teacher who is not inordinately impressed with the sheer logic and beauty of it all, next essays to synthesize it—that is to reduce this chaos to some kind of order. He is not seduced by the magic of all these facts but instead demands relevance. He asks himself, "What, if anything, does all this mean?" This is the next juncture at which the men are separated from the boys. The answer to this question does not come easy. The process of identifying the specific relevance of the subject matter requires native imagination, supplemented by wide reading and another undefinable quality of a good teacher, sensitivity to life and living. The process of isolating the relevance of things is the process of association. Many teachers have little with which to associate; they lack the necessary breadth, particularly required of teachers operating in the area of the humanities. The *answer* to the question of what, if anything, does it all mean? when reduced to a single idea, becomes the basis upon which he launches the development of a lesson plan. The distillation of the idea becomes the *theme* of the lesson providing the direction or thrust of the lesson, the foundation of its unity. He does not confront his class with the step-by-step recounting of the wars by which Rome achieved an empire spreading across the known world, but rather with an idea: that this empire was forged in self defence. When papa asks then, "What did you learn in school today?" instead of the blank look and the feverish scramble through hastily collected notes in search of the dates of the second Punic War, something more emerges, an idea: that Rome conquered the world in self defence. The social studies teacher may be induced to move beyond the historical synthesis to spend his class time in developing the hypothesis that most human aggression is rooted in insecurity. He makes *use* of the original historical subject matter but has not become obsessed with transferring it intact to his students.

In the above instance the teacher has selected one of two possible approaches to his subject matter, electing to develop a concept and to thus demonstrate relevance by *enlarging* the consideration. He has expanded the meaning of the subject matter under his consideration by a macrocosmic handling of his material. This is handled in the domain of the intellect, moving from the particular to the general. The second alternative open to him is to apply a microcosmic approach. Oddly, although his focus in this second instance is upon detail as he contracts the consideration and focuses upon the most minute detail, the final result still has the character of synthesis. He is still reducing chaos to order. The process in this case is not intellectual, but is more properly the attempt to convey an emotional impression. The task of the teacher here is to paint the most minute detail of the historical picture, his final object being an impression of the overall color. The possibility is peculiar to the study of history, though not exclusive to it. Literature teachers make use of the same device in character analysis—projecting, for instance, the character of Eugenie Grandet by the most painstaking inspection of his clothing. The overall impression is brought home through attention to the superficial *minutiae*.

The vivid bombardment with detail that characterizes the books of Bruce Catton drives the reader to an all-consuming interest in the American Civil War even though the day after the reading the detail in which he thrilled is gone—the names of the officers, the caliber of the regiments and their colors and maneuvers—all of this is gone leaving behind vivid general impressions and a giant thirst. The alert teacher who is also a skillful lecturer capitalizes on the tremendous motivational power of the microcosmic treatment of the subject material. How much of the terror of the French Revolution can be projected through a close-up of the insanity of Joseph Fouché (though he is rarely mentioned in standard high school texts)! How much of the spirit of the Reformation is to be captured in re-creating the scene of Luther's appearance before Charles V and accounting for himself: *"Hier stehe Ich, Ich kann nicht anders!"* What matters if the scene is embellished when the overall dramatic impression is the objective? And the teacher must not lose sight of his special objective; he must understand implicitly that the details, so carefully culled, polished and presented, serve only for the instant and then vanish.

The teacher who insists that his lessons be meaningful dialogues or monologues (I don't say *useful* in any hedonistic sense) is a God-send to his students. They credit him with powers of discrimination and are much more disposed to listen to what he has to say. Much of what's wrong with classroom teaching is the fault of teachers who are unconcerned with, or oblivious to, relevance. In this category there are those who *do* ask themselves the question, "What does it all mean?" and answer it with "It doesn't mean anything." Then they go ahead and teach it anyway! It seems that the whole thing is beyond their control. They are really great teachers who are ruthlessly oppressed by the dicta of state education departments, ministries of education and college entrance exams. They are our Prometheans, chained to rocks in the sea lest they should steal fire from the gods and bring it to man. Their art is hampered, if not suppressed, and theirs is the damnation of perpetuating the great mediocrity though they themselves abhor it. There are thousands of them, but for every thousand there is a real teacher somewhere who practices his art before a comparative handful of delighted and very lucky students every year. And they know they're lucky. If there were to be a teaching profession one day, it would be a very exclusive group of people.

With the problem of selection of content and establishment of a theme out of the way, the next difficulty is the setting down of lesson objectives. At this point they have already been formulated in the mind, and the process of putting them down in writing may seem a little needless. Not so: reducing the projected aims to clear crisp statements sorts out the vagueries that may have been blurs in the mental process. Many ideas that seem to be flashes of genius have a way of eluding clear simple expression. Usually the attempt to capture the idea in black and white brings such problems to the surface *before* the teacher undertakes to plot the development of the idea. If the idea is not sound enough, much better to abort early. Certainly, if the idea can't be set down in the calm of preparation, it has little chance of finding effective expression under fire in actual presentation.

Methods texts are fond of classifying objectives in terms of two general areas: the *cognitive* or those relating to the process of intellection, and the *affective* or those relating to whatever it is that has to do with attitudes and values. Emotion? The cognitive aims lend themselves more readily to intelligent definition and discussion than do the affective. These two categories of aims are treated in detail in other chapters of this book. Suffice it for purposes of the present discussion to say that the cognitive aims, classified as those relating to the development of information, understandings and skills require more deliberate attention. The lesson's focus, most commonly, is on the development of understandings. Information, of and by itself, *cannot* serve as the basis for a course, and rarely as the basis for the daily lesson plan. In any case, it is of paramount importance for any teacher, first year or fiftieth, to spell out the lesson objectives concisely and to weigh them very carefully. I have noted in the course of reviewing hundreds of lesson plans, that where objectives are stated in perfunctory fashion and treated with indifference, almost invariably the subsequent development falters badly and finally collapses in total fog.

With the objectives set firmly and clearly, the process of giving the plan a general shape begins. A lesson plan should first be sketched in very roughly in its entirety. More like the water color than the oil painting, quick bold strokes are appropriate to preserving a unity while shaping it. The major ideas to be considered by way of developing the theme become the first focus of attention. Very often the shape of the entire lesson is dictated at once by the definition of the terms contained in the theme. Treating the theme, "The Influences of Geography on the Greek Civilization," the teacher recognizes that he must provide for two basic considerations: A. A Description of Greek Civilization; B. A Description of Greek Geography. Following the intent of his theme, the third major portion of his lesson must provide: C. Demonstration of the

Influence of B upon A. The general plot of the plan has been provided by the theme itself. A further consideration: D. The plays of Aeschylus, would necessarily be rejected as irrelevant to the development of the lesson's theme.

The substructuring takes shape quickly and is governed entirely by the same criterion as the superstructuring; that what is added in the structure must serve the development of the theme. All else is rejected. Of course, theme, superstructure and substructure are essential whether the lesson is to be presented as lecture or inquiry. The so-called "open-end discussion lesson," widely used by teachers (especially on Monday mornings), is characterized by a complete absence of structure, has a tendency to generate more heat than light, and cannot be considered a genuinely instructional experience except under rare circumstances. Development in a lesson does not just happen; it must be provided.

The lesson's conclusion is probably next in line for consideration. Before giving it specific attention, the teacher is well advised to re-check his lesson objectives and then review the lesson's major ideas or superstructure. The conclusion should proceed naturally from the development and clinch the objective. If our lesson's principal objective was for the student "to understand that the geography of a country exercises a direct influence upon the development of its civilization," then an effective summary discussion question might ask, "can you identify the influence that geography has had on any of the modern civilizations with which we are familiar?" The well selected thought question is a most effective way to conclude a lesson since it forces the student to review the theme and to re-apply the intellectual process of the lesson's development in a new situation. After shaping such summary questions, it is useful to glance once more at the lesson's objective—just to make sure.

There remain two tasks: the building in of appropriate homework assignment and the working in of color. The homework
assignment is treated in Chapter Ten. Color is particularly necessary in the fashioning of an introduction to the lesson, which is
capable of getting it off the ground. Often teachers note on
their lesson plan the "materials" that they use in teaching it.
Such lists include good books marked for reading in class, film-
strips, slides showing, for example, the Greek coastline, and
various artifacts and replicas or "props." Let me emphasize at
this point that the teacher should make his materials serve his
purpose, not build his purpose around a good "solid" or gim-
mick. Some teachers have a thing with their audio-visual toys.
There are a good many social studies courses in operation
around the land that would come to an abrupt end if the plug
was pulled out of the wall. Listening to the class's appointed
instructor for ten minutes, however, might prove far worse. At
least with the lights out the kids can sleep.

The following outline, "Some Criteria for Judging the
Mechanics of the Effective Lesson," is designed for evaluating,
not the blueprint of a lesson which has been the subject of our
discussion, but rather the teacher's *execution* of the blueprint
in a live situation. It does not provide a lesson plan format;
almost any methods text in the library does. Nor does it pretend to evaluate the *teacher*. This I leave, with some uncon-
cealed misgivings, to the experts.

## SOME CRITERIA FOR JUDGING
## THE MECHANICS
## OF THE EFFECTIVE LESSON

### THE LESSON

I. Is it informative? (Consideration of the *importance* of the
   subject and the *clarity* of its presentation)

A. Introduction

    1. Is there a *clear statement of the lesson's subject* and *agreed upon definition of its terms?*

    2. Is the *subject's importance* clearly understood?

    3. Is there an attempt to relate the subject to other knowledge?

    4. Is there sufficient overview provided so that the class understands the direction in which the lesson will develop?

B. Development

    1. Are each of the points included in the lesson relevant to the lesson's subject?

    2. Is there a logical progression from point to point?

C. Conclusion

    1. Is there a *clear statement* of what has been demonstrated and how?

    2. Does this *conclusion proceed logically* from the evidence?

    3. Is there opportunity provided to *apply what has been learned* in this lesson in a new situation?

    4. Does the teacher suggest or bring out *further implications* of what has been learned in the lesson?

II. Is it interesting? (Consideration of the *importance* of the subject and the *drama* of its presentation)

A. Is the lesson's subject *worthy* of the attention of one's fellow human beings for three quarters of an hour?

B. Are there *colorful* materials used in advancing the lesson (Great *ideas,* descriptive detail, anecdotal material, maps, readings, pictures, graphic illustration, etc.)? Are they *appropriate* and *well executed?*

# EIGHT

## INQUIRY: TEACHING WITH THE INTELLECT AS TARGET

*If he is indeed wise he does not bid you enter the house of his wisdom, but rather leads you to the threshold of your own mind.*
*Kahlil Gibran*

It is conceivable, is it not, that a student could go through a good many of our junior and senior high school programs in social studies managing quite respectable grades without being required at any time to do any *thinking?* The emphasis is clearly upon memorization and regurgitation of "facts." Such has been the case for far too long. The misplaced emphasis upon memory is an anti-intellectual conspiracy that should have been put to flight with the invention of the printing press. Certainly, by all standards of reason, it should never have survived the paper-back revolution that began to set in immediately following World War II. Even the impact of the mass media has not brought about any appreciable re-alignment of the values that underlie social studies instruction. Students all over the continent are still held responsible for the names of kings and queens, and the dates of the rise and fall of empires, though the material is readily available in books. We continue to insist that education at the fingertips is not as good or as useful somehow as when it has been stored away in the head. We suffer in patience the equating of recall with education, of recitation with learning; even, at the university level, of proper footnoting with research, of mechanics with scholarship. By our hopelessly obsolete instruction techniques, we continue to insist that future problems can be handled by people whose minds are stocked with color-coded information. I risk no exaggeration in pointing out that the memory emphasis continued over a period of time has the effect of deteriorating man's capacity for original thought, for intellectual creativity. This misplaced emphasis that allows the mind to lie fallow is ultimately ruinous. The development of memory has its uses, no doubt, but it is not synonymous with the development of the mind.

The recently resurrected inquiry approach—by which we simply mean the system of beginning with the question instead of assuming the sacrosanctity of the answer—has made something of an impact upon our educational system. The inquiry approach has benefited handsomely from an elaborate publicity campaign which has gone so far in its enthusiasm as to label it it "new." On the North American continent the word "new" has an almost messianic appeal; perhaps this is itself a symptom of the desperation of our situation. While not disavowing the usefulness of publicity, I would much rather see the systematic, though undoubtedly slower, conversion of the teacher to a genuine intellectual appreciation of the value of the inquiry approach. In time, I suspect, even the most recalcitrant among us will come to recognize that we spend far too much time, as Lincoln Steffens lamented, learning the things we already know, and not enough finding out what we don't know. Probably the most potent force in bringing about the dawning of this realization is the sheer immensity of the knowledge explosion. This, more than anything else, combined with the emergence in both prestige and popularity of the social sciences—will generate the reaction against non-think education. If nothing else, we must be cognizant of the physical impossibility of committing all-important knowledge to memory. Even the social scientist dedicated to the most severely specialized area cannot hope to perform such a miracle. Nor would he consider it. Only the student who cannot escape is required to make the attempt.

Apart from any discussion of the impossibility of memorizing everything that we need to know—and so often such information is cloaked in nothing more than the unconvincing garb of "what the educated gentlemen needs to know"—the pedagogical principle involved will not support the memorization approach. What has been "learned" for an examination fades quickly into oblivion once the examination has been written. Entire languages, once mastered, are forgotten in disuse. Instructors who have been teaching the same material for years (alas) find the need for "brushing up" before presenting it in class again. Assuming for the moment that what is being "learned" has value, what remains with the student who has faithfully memorized in class and then departs in June? What remains of his learning? The human memory is so constructed that it will not allow itself to become cluttered. This is why telephone companies publish directories and wives carry grocery lists.

The rise in popularity and prestige of the social sciences and their gradual absorption into the curriculum is another significant factor in the emergence of an inquiry approach. The social sciences force a re-orientation away from the answers and toward the questions. They pose problems that have not yet been explored, and the exploration of these problems produces an effect more gratifying to the teacher and more satisfying to the student than the academic interpretation and re-interpretation of past events.

The hostility to the inquiry approach is in part temperamental and in part reasoned. Temperamentally, it is objectionable because it means scrapping the notes and simple methods that have been used for years by teachers secure in the notion that they have all the answers, and bypassing textbooks based upon the same notion, texts that represent a considerable financial investment. Also there is the natural resistance to giving up an easy way to embrace a more difficult one. Inquiry teaching is hard.

The reasoned hostility usually takes the form of objection to wasting class time. It requires much more time to probe and question students on the meaning of "imperialism" than it does to supply a definition for them to commit to memory. Of this there is no doubt. But which way do they *learn?* Isn't this the paramount consideration of the classroom teacher?

"Education," if we go back to our Latin for a moment, is the process of "leading out." Strange that, in spite of the millions of dollars we spend each year on education, we have lost sight of something the Romans were implicitly aware of. But then they didn't have to meet university admission requirements; they were too busy establishing an empire and providing for its administration. The Socratic method, put to good use in Athens while the Romans were still children, was a contrivance which, through a series of questions, put the mind through a harrowing intellectual process, the net result of which was education. Perhaps it was the original systematic inquiry approach to teaching. More than likely not. But it does provide a handsome historical precedent and its effectiveness is not to be denied. A reading of *The Dialogues* illuminates the nature of the Socratic, or inquiry, method. Let us view it in terms of the teaching objectives classified under the cognitive domain.

The first of these is the objective relating to *information.* This, of course, is the area that we usually emphasize. For us information, of and by itself, has a certain magic and our instruction technique is a ritualistic tribute to its importance. Yet the students of Socrates found that what they recalled quickly enough when pressed with a question would not satisfy the old man who pushed them back further upon themselves. He refused to accept what was advanced on authority, accepting only what could be demonstrated. Most social studies courses that I've seen rely in greatest part, if not exclusively, upon a textbook. What fun Socrates might have had with any one of them! I have guided candidates for the master's degree who relax confidently in the citing of a precedent for their ideas and feel no compulsion beyond this to defend them. A bibliography has become accepted as adequate justification for acceptance—a substitute for thinking. To press for a definition of terms other than the hand-me-down is an unspeakable affront not only to the student but to the integrity of past scholarship—a form of genuine anti-intellectualism. The present credulity of students is a species of superstition that we as teachers have allowed and encouraged. All teachers and students should be sworn to an educational Hippocratic Oath.

I am not arguing that information is of no importance, but rather that it has no intrinsic importance apart from incorporation into the *thinking* of an individual. The value of information resides exclusively in its assimilation into the intellectual make-up of a human being. Its value, apart from relation to the intellectual processes, simply does not exist. In our own instruction technique, information has become a grotesque master rather than slave. The genuine inquiry method will not permit this, but demands, by its very nature, that information be relegated to its proper place in the intellectual process. The inquiry approach is an intellectual process.

The function of the inquiry approach is to make use of information in developing *understanding*. The understanding, because it is integrally bound up in the intellectual process, has a permanence which unrelated information does not enjoy. A man's understandings become a part of himself and the basis of further learning. Socrates establishes the understanding and then moves *a priori* to further understandings. The process is unending. The process of understanding is a genuinely intellectual process involving the recognition of the identity or non-identity between two concepts. Understanding is the apprehension of relationship. The soul of the teaching of understandings is a demonstration of the relevance of information, of single concepts. The function of the teacher using the inquiry approach is to bring the single concepts of the student into such a position that the student is compelled to posit or negate a relationship existing between them, and then to define what that relationship is. Forcing such connections is a very tricky business and it is this that requires such careful attention to the plotting of the superstructure and substructure in the development of the lesson, as mentioned in the previous chapter.

When the student is directly and personally involved in establishing his own connections between distinct ideas, be they negative or affirmative, he understands. When the teacher makes the connections for him as in the lecture method, student's intellectual process has not necessarily been involved. He arrives at no understanding by being told; he is simply provided with more information without benefit of firsthand experience of its relevance necessary to make it a part of his learning.

The final cognitive objective, the development of *skills,* involves learning through application. Through application of learning in new and unfamiliar situations, the student tests the strength of his understanding. Beyond this he tests its reliability and is afforded the opportunity of making any necessary modifications. The development of skills is an essential part of anchoring the newly-won understanding. The teacher cannot afford to ignore this facet of instruction. It is accomplished through a process of more questions deliberately calculated to push the student beyond the now familiar ground where he developed the understanding and, as before, move him further into the unfamiliar. The inquiry approach is "pushy." (Socrates was executed.) At this point the teacher is introducing new variables in an effort to unseat the understanding, to throw the hound off the track. The purpose of the inquiry approach is to equip the student, both temperamentally and intellectually, to handle even a situation totally foreign to him. The emphasis is off the familiar and onto the unfamiliar; off the answers and onto the questions; off comfort and onto disturbance. Instead of being handed cut flowers, the student is being shown how to plant.

The inquiry approach is tough. There are no two ways about it. It's tougher on the teacher and it's tougher on the students. Few of us want to use any concentration or start monkeying around with thinking if education can be done as well some other way. The problem is that it can't. We've got to re-examine what it is that we're doing to these people under the guise of instructing them, and we've got to pull them off pablum and put them on meat. And we must do all this *now*.

The supreme accomplishment of the inquiry approach is that it trains students how to think and it gets them into the habit of thinking. When the teacher's target is the intellect, which is not always the case, the inquiry approach is a natural. The inquiry approach introduces the student (and usually the teacher who has been bold enough to try it) to the process of understanding or learning on a step-by-step basis beginning with observations, and proceeding through the drawing of inferences from these observations, the formulation of hypotheses respecting what we have observed and inferred, and testing the reliability of these hypotheses. Finally, the student should be encouraged to apply his hypotheses by projecting the future dimensions of whatever situation has been under observation. Since the proper object of the social scientist's concern is man in his relations with other men, or simply man in society, then for us, as social studies teachers, the situation under observation will be a group of people located in time and space. As will be demonstrated in the next chapter, the society need not necessarily be real to begin with.

The first step in the process is to *observe*. People, excepting police and others specially trained, do not observe things. Yet this is the pediment upon which all other knowledge rests. "For nothing is so productive of elevation of mind," Aurelius tells us, "as to be able to examine methodically and truly every object which is presented to thee. . . ." Developing this power in ourselves, or helping to develop it in others is very exciting— partly, I'm convinced, because of the sheer novelty of it all. It is exciting from its earliest stage where we discover the world of difference between seeing and observing, that to see is not to observe, reminding us of Thoreau's concentration on an ant hill until a universe unfolded itself before his eyes.

In my own class I have introduced the problem of learning to observe by providing each student with an empty cigarette box and a hypothetical situation. "You are an archaeologist working on the site of this ancient city in the year 3000 AD. You have unearthed the artifact you now hold in your hand. What do you observe of this earlier society?" I stand at the board, chalk in hand, with two things to do: list the observations as they pour forth (from any age group), and to remind them to relate their observation to man. He is our focal point. It is not as useful to observe that the package is red as to observe that man had the use of red. It is also necessary from time to time to disallow inference from the observations. Discussion and experimentation with the processes of deduction I reserve for later in the week. We are concerned at this point with direct sense perception. The list of observations mounts quickly to a startling number.

In a follow-up lesson with the class I begin by replacing the list on the board (the janitor always erases our work or I've used the board to do the same thing with another class), and then invite the students to recognize the need for some system of classification for our observations. The three major questions, the superstructure of the day's lesson, are usually *Would it be useful to classify our observations somehow?* (If there are a good many observations, this may occur to them without their being asked.) *What purpose would be served by classifying our observations?* (Substructure questioning should bring out at least two: for distinguishing and for ordering our information.) *How does one go about devising a system of classification?* Here we want the student to establish the basis of classification. (Substructure questions plus trial and error bring out the point that a good classification system has two qualities: it must be comprehensive and its parts must be as distinct as possible.) We usually arrive at the political, economic and social (or cultural) breakdown as the basis for classifying what we observe.

Connected with the question of observation is the question of sources. There needs to be some new thought here since the idea of social studies inquiry and the idea of textbook are contradictory notions. If we start off with the answers, there's little point to further inquiry. What is needed is some plentiful, constant and inexpensive supply of sources from which we can collect evidence of man, or particular groups of men, in action. Such sources, unlike resourceful teachers, are limitless. Class subscription (being careful not to duplicate the library's) to good newspapers and respectable magazines from around the world would be a good beginning. The UNESCO *Courier* contains the sort of thing that is needed. Delegations to the U.N. and foreign consulates (somewhat less so) are often happy to oblige students with information on the origins, development, problems and dreams of their people. The most anxious to help are the very nations whose involvement in "critical" situations make them most demanding of our attention. Care must be taken not to overload the political and economic aspects to the exclusion of the cultural. There are several new magazines on African Art, for example, that should find their way into an exciting program. Radio and television are particularly useful. And of course there is the aforementioned limitless possibility of the use of novels.

I know that there are teachers who, in the midst of all this postwar source explosion, throw up their hands and wail that there aren't enough sources to support such a program of instruction. Nothing surprises me anymore.

After some practice in observing and classifying what is observed, the teacher might next introduce the process of deductive thinking or drawing inferences from our observations. Having introduced the term "deduction," I will now abandon it (it's slippery) in favor of "inference." The most satisfactory way I've discovered of teaching the nature and beauty of the inference process is to read selections illustrating the process from Sherlock Holmes stories. What more captivating and graphic example is there than the master sleuth recounting step by step to an astonished Watson, the working of his active mind. In my own class I present a paperback edition of Doyle's famous tales to the student who can infer the greatest number of logical possibilities from a single shred of evidence. I have found that such added encouragement is not required. But I do it anyway. Part of the excitement for a teacher is to stop the natural mental process at each phase so that the whole class may examine the nature of each process and work on developing each one.

For example, the mind leaps naturally to the hypothesis even from a single observation. The hypothesis or generalization is among the most formidable of the teacher's weapons because it serves two uses. It is, first, a station at which we can recoup; at which we can collect and organize our observations and inferences, thus renewing our sense of direction and our courage. Second, a hypothesis by its very nature seduces man into a renewal of the struggle. It is not an answer. It is *an* explanation for what we have observed—still very much a question. It is not yet either right or wrong. It is challenging, romantic and exciting. "The error of a great man," wrote Nietzche to his sister, "is more venerable than the truths of a thousand little men." With the creation of the hypothesis, right or wrong, the student has now hurtled beyond the perimeter of what is known.

Testing the hypothesis may be an *a priori* check of its validity, or, as is more often the case, a check against the concrete phenomena that will confirm or refute it. Most of our hypotheses are yielded by the process of induction, that is, reasoning from a number of particular instances to a general truth. Because the social scientist has the dimension of history at his disposal, a number of tests are readily available. At this point, in order to maintain our scientific posture, we must encourage the student to re-double the guard against subjectivity. Then we start back through history in search of specific situations that will test the reliability of our theory. But history does have the happy tendency of proving those hypotheses that we're fond of, and disproving the less exciting ones. Even the social science hypothesis, which by virtue of its generic nature should transcend the narrower concerns that constitute so many historical interpretations, is invested with special armament by the ego of the individual who developed it. This must be prepared for; I doubt that it can be resolved. But this is the process of thinking itself, and when the target of the teacher is the intellect few devices are more appropriate than the question.

The key to the success or failure of the inquiry approach as introduced into the individual classroom is the teacher's talent for questioning. An effective questioning technique is crucial. There is a happy note to be sounded when talking about the development of a human being's questioning technique: it can be done. Teachers who are ineffective lecturers come by it naturally, even though they can be improved to some extent. Since the usual basis of the difficulty is personality, the subject is better advised to develop something else in its place. The questioning technique does not involve the vexing personality mysteries and the largely ineffectual can, with training, become quite masterful teachers. Little or any drama is required— clarity is the main virtue—and the clod who demonstrates any imagination at all in conjunction with an alert mind has pos- sibilities. Unfortunately, a mind is still essential; in fact, more so.

The fact that there is such comparatively little use of the inquiry approach suggests that it involves a special knack, and that teachers are not being encouraged—much less instructed— in developing it. Once developed, and it can be developed with little if any outside help, the use of the inquiry adds a vitality that very often diminishes for the lecturer after just one or two years of teaching, The teacher who uses the inquiry method can stay alive intellectually indefinitely; no two years, no two classes, no two students are ever the same. Every teaching experience is unique.

Before going on to shed what I am afraid is very little light on the process of developing the questioning technique, I would attempt to describe it. I did not say "define" it. In examining questions that teachers raise in classrooms it is necessary to distinguish at least two things: their quality and the number in which they occur. In relation to the former, the quality of the question, we are distinguishing between eliciting recitation and genuine probing; between a question that induces recall and a question that makes the human being itch. "What was the year of *Magna Carta?*" will not make a student uncomfortable. He merely gives back something that's been given him (which he had no use for anyway); he has not been forced to give up part of himself. The education courses treating this point distinguish between "what" and "why" questions. This, of course, is an artificial distinction that probably messes up as many teachers as it helps. The theory is that recall questions usually begin with the word "what," and that "thought" questions begin with "why." But as many questions as not that begin with the word "why" are purely and simply recall questions. On the other hand, we are told that Pilate asked Christ, "What is truth?" which would seem to have demanded something more than recall. We have need of a more substantive distinction. Pursuing the above point, it would seem that when the teacher does *not* have the answer, or what he thinks is the answer, the quality of his question is likely to be quite high. The superb question forces the student into a confrontation; he must confront himself, not consult his textbook. The superb question triggers a dialogue within the minds of the questioned and of the questioner. Such questions fall like bombs; people within the sound of the explosion generally take notice. After a few of these the teacher finds himself learning along with the students. The prig, of course, finds this intolerable.

The problem of the number of questions is also important in describing the character of questioning. In classroom recitation the ordinary process is to spray the questions over the lot, hitting as many individuals as possible. The individual's answer to any one of the questions makes little difference. There is no process. There is no development. Similarly, if a question is left out, nothing is lost. Good questioning technique involves process and development like the Socratic dialogue. Questions are used here in combinations. In the chess game one move may or may not be telling, but the combination moves provide inescapable consequences. The same is true of boxing and of the questioning technique. The peculiarity of process questioning, as distinguished from recitation questioning, is that each question is shaped by the preceding response, and related to the previous and subsequent questions. Since this building process is going on, the teacher has to adjust himself to actually listening to the answers that are given to his questions. This is novel. It also results very quickly in a general improvement of the questions asked and the answers given. Under such circumstances neither the teacher nor the students can remain oblivious to the exchange that is going on between them. The result is human dialogue and it's very stimulating.

In the two preceding paragraphs I have already ventured into the first and most important consideration of the teacher who wants to develop an effective questioning technique. This is a consideration of teacher temperament. The teacher who's going to try the inquiry approach on any sustained basis has to be the kind of person who can admit to himself, *and before others when necessary,* that he doesn't know all there is to know. Beyond this—in the case especially of teachers who've been lecturing for twenty years—that perhaps what they do know isn't as important as they might have assumed. This is a tough prescription. The primary ingredient is a genuine intellectual humility conceived and sustained in the recognition of how little we know. But how many of us have not yet reached even this point. A certain amount of trepidation seems much more appropriate to the teacher than the smug little confidence in his own accumulation of trivia. The teacher is every bit as much the student as those whom he pretends to instruct. The first and most difficult obstacle to hurdle in developing a questioning technique involves a particularly unpleasant but exciting intellectual overhaul of basic values. We must dispose ourselves to let go of the piling and strike out for the deepest part, and to take the students with us.

Academically, the thing of most value in developing questioning technique is to familiarize ourselves with the basic principles of logic, to practice applying them to our own thought and to insist upon logical thought processes from our students. Far too often the social studies class sails into full debate of a proposition like "If he's old enough to fight, he's old enough to vote," in blithe disregard of the complete dissimilarity of the two predicates. A logic course is useful if available, and were I dean of a faculty of education I would require a logic course for all candidates for teaching careers. A formal course however is not necessary; there are several excellent, inexpensive texts available that can be mastered in the quiet of one's own room. One I have found particularly useful is Robert J. Kreyche's *Logic for Undergraduates* (Holt, Rinehart, Winston, 1954).

The most important thing, in fact, is an awakened interest that will force our attention to logical processes. There's no point in memorizing the kinds of syllogisms or the squares of opposition. What we need to do is to pay attention, particularly to definitions. Care exercised in the working out of definitions is the greatest exercise in developing logical thinking habits. A good number of social studies lessons should revolve around nothing but definition. A forty-five minute period is little enough time to allow students to produce a working definition of the term "imperialism." The order of the lesson:

1. Tell them that we're going to try to evolve a satisfactory definition of imperialism. Demonstrate that the ones that we have conflict.
2. Have them suggest the names of "imperial" powers, and put the names of these on the board. (At least a half dozen.
3. Have them describe for each of the powers listed the

specific act by which they have identified this power as "imperialistic." Here is the place to insist upon precision and specifics.

4. Have them distinguish any different *kinds* of imperialism. If there is difficulty suggest that they examine the motives behind the acts.

5. Once distinguishing between political, economic and cultural "imperialism," have students produce more examples of each of the three to be sure that the difference between them is anchored.

6. Have them sort out the elements that are common to all three; and list these elements on the board.

7. Have them discuss each of the elements in turn to see if there is agreement or disagreement as to (1) whether element *is* common to all three, (2) whether element then is *essential* part of a definition.

8. Have students at their desks work the remaining elements on the board into a concise written definition.

9. Single out the best of these and put up on board for approval. Get two or three and have class tell which they like best and why.

But when do they find out that Cecil Rhodes was born in 1853 and died in 1902? They don't.

The final thing that I'd like to mention as having to do with the questioning technique I do not understand at all. I include it because it is curious and I am confident that it cannot be "researched." Somehow it might be helpful to a teacher. If we could assume for the moment that a lesson's presentation was a photograph, the lecture approach would be, if you will, the print. The inquiry approach bears somehow the same relationship to the lecture that the negative does to the print. The teacher who is to present in inquiry fashion must shift his interest from print to negative and get used to working in reverse. As Cézanne demonstrated to the world of art, if you will project an apple, the trick is not to paint the apple, but to paint the area around the apple. It seems to me that our trick then calls for projecting the conclusions as we find them by defining the space around them. This seems to be the function of the question.

# NINE

## LECTURE: TEACHING
## WITH THE WILL AS TARGET

The most popular method of instruction at the college and
secondary level for centuries has been the lecture method. It
has survived the advent of the printing press, the paperback
revolution, an explosion in mass media, and the repeated as-
saults of a legion of quixotic pedagogues who lecture tirelessly
on its evils and obsolescence. Its struggle against this formidable
array of natural enemies has made it, if anything, hardier.
Classroom teachers confess to me when out of earshot of student teachers, "I know the method is in some disrepute but,
well, you know. . . ." In New York City where the lecture's
disrepute is formal enough to be reckoned with, many teachers
proceed with the normal course of instruction but keep a
"developmental" lesson in the drawer against the unannounced
visit of a supervisor. For any or all of the official disenchantment with it, the lecture method will undoubtedly continue as
the dominant method of teaching. Our children and grand-
children will be laid to rest under the echoes of a lecture. As
long as teaching is basically a human to human communication,
and as long as our basic definition of education remains un-
changed, the lecture will hold sway.

The one thing that will drive the lecture method into obscurity is the general abandonment of our present stress upon information and the wholehearted endorsement of the superior value of teaching *how* to think rather than *what* to think. Where the proper function of instruction is seen to be *education* in its real sense, the lecture must die a natural death. But the realization that telling is not teaching comes very hard. We believe rather that what we have to say is of importance, and that once it's been told, it's been taught. Apart from the first assumption—which yields incidentally the chronological survey of history so familiar in our educational system and which is basically incorrect—the second assumption is based not so much upon ignorance as upon laziness. The lecture method persists, in spite of its most obvious inadequacy, because it is purely and simply the easiest way to "teach." We are maintaining that we have no time to *teach* and we are preoccupied instead with "covering ground." Coverage is *not* important and, if it were, "coverage" by lecture method is an illusion. Such coverage as we pretend is demanded by examinations can be done in from four to six weeks. Nothing more detailed will "stick" anyway. The idea that history is somehow "coverable" does violence to the integrity of history and raises havoc with a good teacher's conscience. Once rid of the coverage myth, we are rid of the pre-eminence of the lecture and are ready to begin teaching. Maybe it's time we *un*covered something.

Lecturing is like writing free verse poetry: it's the easiest to do, and the hardest to do *well*. Success in lecturing is conditioned by three factors: the ability of the sender, the willingness and capacity of the receiver, and the nature of the message to be communicated.

In the first instance, it should be pointed out that much of the odium that attaches to the lecture method in "capital E" education circles is the result of a recognition that lectures are ineffective. Some people are just plain dull. Their conversation is dull. They are dull in their living rooms, they are dull at cocktail parties and they are dull in the classroom. There are many reasons. The most basic and inescapable is that they lack personality. For this reason methods classes, courses in oral interpretation of literature, or speech clinics cannot produce effective lectures. Many students of mine have deliberately enrolled in drama programs, but it was their personalities that led them to do it. For this reason alone they were almost invariably better lecturers than those who did not. Undoubtedly a large part of this mysterious "personality" factor is nothing more than awareness of audience, more commonly, "ham." There is more to the great actor than technique and so it is with the lecturer. Apart from the fact that some people are good story tellers and others are not, there is the fact that many would-be lecturers have no story to tell. Successful lecturing is greatly enhanced by wide reading, interest in *ideas* and imagination. Many high school and college instructors have none of these things going for them. Instead they have a sheaf of notes that they have gleaned, in their earnestness, from primary sources. This they expect, along with one or two canned jokes carefully typed into the manuscript, will carry the day. Wrong again. Much "lecturing" is nothing more than a repetition of the textbook. The assumption here is that the student is illiterate. This drives the student to a frenzy and he soon gives up either reading the text, or attending the lectures, or both. Where repeating the text is the case, as it so often is, the instructor is better off calling off his class and assigning a date for an examination on the textbook.

There are a few great lecturers—a handful. They are all masterful; they are artists. Fair to middlin' lecturers are deadly and, with rare exceptions as mentioned in the preceding essay, their ineptitude unfortunately remains a secret only to themselves. In order to justify lecturing, the instructor has to be able to give his students more in an hour's time than they could have got by devoting as much time to reading. Obviously, this brings the would-be lecturer into some pretty stiff competition. He's got to be better than Theodore Mommsen on the Gracchus brothers, better than Charles Dickens on the impact of the English industrial revolution, better than Francis Parkman on the conspiracy of Pontiac, better than Prescott on the conquest of Mexico. In more than twenty-five years of schooling, I have had *one* such teacher; his courses were miracles. And in twenty-five years of schooling I have had nothing *but* lecturers.

The second factor, the capacity and willingness of people to listen well, is a factor that invites our attention to defining our audience more carefully than we have. One estimate puts the span of concentration of the average tenth grader at between eight and twelve minutes, yet full period lectures at this and earlier levels are not uncommon. My own experience corroborates the idea that the student's capacity for absorption is exhausted long before I've come to the end. The idea that any speaker could hold his listeners' attention for a full forty minutes, day after day, compounds the absurdity. As the students' capacity is reached their willingness to concentrate diminishes quickly. At this point all is lost; but the teacher, undaunted, presses on with Alexander for Persepolis, and the bell.

Hand in hand with the lecture method goes encouragement of the students to take notes. Note taking adds a new dimension of ennui to an already tedious process. It almost necessarily precludes any possibility of a student's becoming interested, and sustaining an interest, in what is being said. Many teachers carefully collect and inspect the notebook at the end of the unit and award marks according to how like the textbook the notes are. Such monkish copy work, of course, is useless and amounts to malicious mischief on the part of a teacher. Note taking in history class (the science class—recording procedure and results—is a very different matter) is not so much the "skill" it is purported to be, but a disease. If the teacher would develop a skill in note taking among students, and at the same time increase their capacity and willingness for absorption, let him require that all of the notes from a given lecture are to be recorded on the inside of a matchbook cover. Let this be our definition of coverage. If I had taken a single matchbook cover upon which to record my notes from all of my history courses from high school through graduate school, I would still have plenty of room on it to record any salient ideas that might emerge in post-doctoral courses. For the rest I have books. Note taking has become a substitute for thinking.

Successful lecturing is contingent finally upon the subject matter. The simple fact here, and the general theme of what we have said in earlier chapters, is that what we're offering in social studies classes is not worth recording. What is the *purpose* of re-stating, recording and reciting the dates of the Punic wars? Is it the hope that we are writing them into our minds? Why? When the subject matter is the past, and when our aim is coverage, the lecture method is a total failure—in its conception, in its process, and in its outcome. The massive historical ignorance of the general public is irrefutable proof of its failure. The large scale lecture method is even less suited, if possible, to a social studies program.

To point up the general futility of the lecture method is not to say that at no time is it ever a useful instructional technique. To define the lecture loosely as "teacher-talk" as distinguished from "kid-talk," there are occasions when the teacher is well advised to do the talking. An obvious example is when there is need for specific technical instruction as in the instance of explaining a class assignment.

But beyond this sort of use, there is a quite distinct and very intriguing aspect of instruction for which the lecture device is perfectly suited, and for which no other technique can do as well. We have attempted to suggest in the previous chapter that when the teacher's objective is the development of under-standings, his most proper approach is one of inquiry. The inquiry approach involves the students intellectually. The suc-cessful teacher undertakes to involve his students emotionally as well. It is readily admitted at this point that successful intel-lectual involvement generates its own emotional involvement; that is to say that the more we know, the more we want to know. Learning breeds motivation. But further than this, the teacher of rare gift can attack the affective area directly, rele-gating the development of cognitive powers to a position of secondary importance. His more immediate target becomes the student's interest or, for want of a better word, his will. He is undertaking to inculcate a value, an attitude or an appreciation. We are not pretending that the student's intellect is not involved in the process. Certainly the attitude that should emerge from the lesson of the good Samaritan cannot do so without a basic understanding of the events. We must understand that the Jews and the Samaritans were intensely hostile to one another in order to receive the full appreciation of the Samaritan's gener-osity. The lesson is not important, however, for promoting this understanding; it is an important lesson in what it *does* to us. The Rabbi's target was the emotions of his listeners. When the teacher's target is the emotions, the weapon that he chooses, *if he is gifted in its use,* is the lecture. Or to make the word more palatable to educators and to bring it in closer to our illustration at the same time, "narrative."

Why? Let us begin with an understanding of the peculiar character of the *good* lecture. Lectures, we have said already, are not good when their object is to "cover ground." This sort (the most common) bounces from event to event, like a madman in a flaming straitjacket, without rhyme or reason. The peculiar character of the good lecture is that it comes out somewhere. Every part of the good lecture has a developmental function that contributes to an overall unity. Every part is specifically geared to create one effect, such as "love thy neighbor." If any of these parts are omitted from the good lecture, the effect may not come across. Omitted parts of the "coverage" lecture usually make no difference and will not be missed. This character of the good lecture may be described as the quality of *synthesis*. Synthesis makes the lecture appropriate to developing an emotional impact because synthesis includes the notion of unity. But the well constructed inquiry approach is not random either; it, too, has unity. True, but it may or may not culminate in one specific impact. In an inquiry approach the teacher is forced off the main tack and out onto tangents. There are thirty minds attempting to take the lead, not just one. The one desired effect may easily be lost, and successful engagement of the emotions depends upon the systematic development of *one* effect. Emotional effect is lost in wandering to and from the design. In addition, the inquiry approach necessarily focuses upon the intellect for its development. It is the non-involvement of intellect that makes the lecture or monologue so apt a medium for propaganda. Open dialogue would have ruined Joseph Goebbels or Adolf Hitler. But as they capitalized on non-think monologue for achieving their ends, and with incredible effectiveness, so can the same medium be pressed into service for good. A continuing emotional bombardment of the love-thy-brother message will go much further in public education (because most of us are C-students) than the careful intellectual analysis of racial problems. One social studies class of my experience had the problem of racial tension all nicely ironed out academically, and the unit examination showed a thorough understanding of the biological, legal and moral equality of two races. But six weeks of work went up in smoke when a minority group family moved into the town. In short their understanding collapsed in the face of their inbred attitudes, values and appreciations. Viable instruction must go deeper than the cognitive domain, and there are few teachers equipped to carry it there. Nor can they be produced.

The major heresy of this essay is that the intellectual development of the public may well not be our most important concern; the basic concern of future public education may well be with programming (conditioning, if you prefer) the individual to make the desired, socially accepted response. Certainly this conditioning already underlines our operations in the cognitive area (though the exponents of academic freedom abhor the idea), but such attention to the affective development of human beings may become *de rigueur*. At present such conditioning is sporadic, unstructured, and probably underemphasized.

When the emotional effect becomes the key consideration, truth as we conceive it, that is, as the proper object of the intellect and the elusive fox in the great educational hunt, necessarily becomes expendable. Great lecturers, as well as the authors of great books, have already made the sacrifice. "I would willingly sacrifice the minor fact," says the candid Macaulay, "for the balance of a sentence." The lecturer, driving for an emotional effect must confront the same situation often enough, and undoubtedly must make his concessions. Are we sure that in making the concession that the *truth* has been injured? Or just our commitment to it? Is there not a greater truth than von Ranke's "the way it (history) actually happened?" Is the only truth an intellectual truth?

In addition to these two considerations of the lecture as the more suitable medium for involving students emotionally—the fact that it does not ordinarily entail intellectual involvement and that it does lend itself more readily to accomplishment of pre-conceived unity—it peculiarly affords the opportunity for development of other dramatic effects. The teacher who is emotionally committed becomes impatient with the plodding of students (his commitment compels him to focus upon his subject and not his students) and finds that his personality drives in to support his conviction. Like the wild horse, he must run. He has no alternative but to dominate. (I'm talking about teachers—not saints.) The lecture has a rhythm (lacking of course in ordinary dialogue) which becomes, in the instance of an effective speaker, hypnotic. In the instance of the more familiar ineffective speaker it becomes somnolent. The lecture method provides the occasion for spellbinding, making use of colorful imagery and the proper dramatic pauses, and the teacher himself is likely to be caught up in it.

But alas most lecturers are not spellbinders and cannot become such. The writing on the wall at present indicates that the lecturer will eventually be phased out of social studies instruction because his chosen method is inappropriate to the task as we read it. Once the universities have lumbered into position, they will turn out the teacher equipped to inquire of their students and to involve them intellectually more successfully. But the last of the good lecturers will never be replaced. The blessing comes with the replacement of the rest of them.

# TEN

## HOMEWORK: UNEXPLOITED
## TEACHER RESOURCE

A professor in a large western university, annoyed by the fact
that a rangy, sprawling cowboy regularly slept through his
lectures, paused in the middle of his delivery one afternoon, ad-
dressed a pointed question to his class and then attached the
cowboy's name to the end of it. The cowboy's response reflected
that in his after lunch slumber he had missed the sense of the
discourse. The professor, further annoyed, ventured the observation that the cowboy was better fed than he was educated.
"That may be," drawled his target, "I feed myself and you
educate me." The educational process does not take place
where the student remains uninvolved, regardless of how sweaty
the teacher becomes. The essence of effective teaching, as we
have suggested, is seeing to it that the students are involved.
Students must be deliberately involved and one of the important
ways of involving them is to assign work for which each of them
is personally, directly and individually responsible. Ultimately
what a student gets out of his schooling is what he himself puts
into it—little more, little less. Students will get more out of
carrying out a carefully planned homework assignment than
they do from sitting through a thoroughly planned and magnifi-

cently delivered lecture. As the necessity of student involvement in any genuine educational experience dawns upon us with the impact and surprise of an explosion, we will be forced as teachers to renew our attention to the nature and importance of homework. Strangely, the value of the homework assignment both to students and to teacher actually passes many of us unnoticed. There are probably no teachers who fully exploit on a regular basis the latent power of homework assignments as a learning experience, and no students who regularly reap the learning value of carrying out a well-planned homework assignment.

At the same time there are hordes of teachers who sit around the faculty room complaining about how little time they have in which to present their material to the class. "How can I be expected to cover world history from that day to this? There isn't enough time!" Yet these are often the same teachers who slop through homework assignments in the most perfunctory fashion, thereby failing to take advantage of a factor that would fairly double (at the least) their teaching time. The scene is a familiar one: the bell ending class sounds, the kids' books have been stacked for five minutes (they're not about to make note of anything) and as the teacher comes to and calls out their "homework assignment," half of them are out the door and down the hall. The teacher shrugs and thinks, "Well, it wasn't important anyway; besides they wouldn't have done it." He's probably right on both counts. But, if each of thirty students had been properly required to put in one hour's time on a carefully constructed homework assignment (which the teacher could have engineered in five minutes) the teacher would have doubled his teaching time. Taking five minutes to present the homework assignment sensibly plus the few moments to prepare it, would have netted a collective return of thirty hours of application to his subject by his class. Instead, day after day we write it off out of sheer carelessness and inattention.

A second bonus that we write off by slopping through meaningless or routine homework assignments involves another aspect of the time factor. When material is covered adequately by students preparing a homework assignment, it need not and indeed *should* not be covered again in class. The teacher is thus released to do something with his class that will reinforce what they've learned on their own, or interest them in tackling something else. Class periods that had been devoted to coverage are then released for discussion, reinforcement, topics of interest and greater depth. In some painful cases, however, the instructor guarantees his material coverage by carefully assigned and checked homework assignments, but then instead of enticing the students into developing a real interest, spends the class sessions going over the homework. The professorial variation is to assign the reading in the text for homework, then to read it to the students for class without changing a word. Very quickly the student gets the idea; he won't do any reading because the prof lectures on the same thing in class. Next, he discovers he doesn't need to go to class because he's got all the material in the text. The net result is that he does neither. Maybe he finds his way to the library in search of some intellectual stimulation or, more likely, he just sleeps in.

Few teachers enjoy teaching students who are unprepared. When they are prepared they will carry the class themselves when given half a chance, and the teacher will find his job a piece of cake. And the thing is a delicious circle; when they find they enjoy their class, they are more disposed to do more work; when they find their class is a drag, they also find they're not much interested in doing their outside assignments either. It appears then, that apart from the very important time consideration, the homework question and its handling can either make or break a class.

It can also make or break a teacher. According to at least one survey, the principal reason why first-year teachers leave the field is because they were unable to control the situation, i.e., discipline problems. Few discipline problems arise in situations where the class is enjoying its work; where they are not, they have recourse to enjoying themselves or, in certain horrible situations, to enjoying the teacher. Any student enjoys a class for which he has prepared; few enjoy classes for which they have not prepared. I can remember *not being able to wait* to get to Latin class on mornings for which I knew my vocabulary and grammar cold, and had prepared my translation. On the days that I was not prepared, my first reaction was to cut the class. When this failed, I attended physically only, dreading that I would be called upon next, afraid of stirring or looking up at the teacher. The teacher owes it to the student and to himself to see to it that the student is prepared. In the high school class students who come into the room unprepared can have an immediate and disastrous effect. In large numbers they become impatient with the teacher and with the few who may have attempted preparation. As they become increasingly restive, the teacher, who is depending upon class participation to carry his lesson at least in part, has a first class discipline problem on his hands. Because of homework assignments mindlessly constructed and sloppily given, students get less than half the education they might get, teachers get a fraction of the cooperation students would be happy to give, the subject area hasn't a chance to make any friends or even acquaintances for itself, and quantities of time, energy and money go down the drain.

In order to capitalize on the value of homework as an ally to the teacher and student, the teacher must be adept at constructing and assigning homework, and at making sure that the homework is done. The homework assignment must be conceived and created in full and clear view of the intended purpose it will serve. A common problem is that there isn't any purpose either for the teacher, or for the students. Homework is assigned and completed (when students take the trouble) without purpose or meaning, and purely as a matter of routine. Few things inhibit learning as quickly and as completely as routinizing it. Kids copy written homework papers without the idea of personal value even occurring to them. If written homework is to be assigned, there must be a reason for it, some predetermined objective to be accomplished by having the student actually write something. If that objective would be served as well by the student's reading, then there is no reason for his writing homework. When the teacher has no particular reason for assigning homework, then presumably he has no basis of evaluating the job the student has done. I have sat in class after class where the teacher has forgotten to pick up completed homework assignments. The indication is that such an activity was purposeless. If the teacher forgets it, can he reasonably expect that his students will continue to take it seriously? All homework must have a purpose. Kids don't need extra "Mickey Mouse" work to do any more than their teachers do. Homework assignments must be planned with objectives clearly in mind in the same way that effective units, lessons and examinations are planned.

Once the teacher has set an assignment with which he is pleased, that is, convinced that it provides a substantial learning experience designed to achieve a particular end, he next plots the presentation of the assignment. It is not enough to write the week's assignments in one corner of the board which the students are to copy into their notes without benefit of any explanation. Such a procedure quickly defeats itself. Instead the teacher carefully constructs the presentation of the assignment for his class with a deliberation that reflects its importance. In constructing that presentation he concerns himself with four major questions.

The first question to be treated is what is to be done. Once the teacher knows what he wants done, he must present it clearly and explicitly. Many assignments end in failure because the student is not clear as to exactly what is expected of him. The chances are that the teacher who tells his students that "For tomorrow, I want you to read President Lincoln's Gettysburg Address," does not know what he wants. Nor will his students have any clue. Because it is not specific as it stands, the students still don't know what to do and, technically, no assignment has been given. On the following day, the teacher undertakes to check to see whether the kids have "done their assignment," and he starts them off with a quiz: "In his Gettysburg Address, Mr. Lincoln indicates three causes of the Civil War. List the three on a piece of paper and hand it in." The students, as should be expected, look at each other in mild surprise. The teacher becomes incensed with their reaction, concludes that they have not done their homework, and realizes that he has no base of understanding upon which to build his day's lesson. The point is that he should have been as specific in stating what he wanted from his students' reading of the address when he assigned the reading. The time for him to indicate the specific context of the reading was when it was assigned. In terms of *what* he wanted done, his homework assignment was incomplete. The student who had not bothered to read the address is no more disadvantaged than the student who read it three times. The teacher is entirely at fault.

He should have indicated as part of his assignment, (1) the circumstances in which Mr. Lincoln delivered the address, (2)

what Mr. Lincoln was attempting to do, and (3) his feeling
that Mr. Lincoln suggested in the address what he felt were
three causes for the American Civil War. He then should have
charged his students to find them. Technically this would have
constituted an assignment. Students should never be charged
with reading something without being told what the reading is
about, and what exactly they are to look for. Many teachers
assign pages of a textbook for reading without knowing exactly
what is in the text. The assignment runs, "For tomorrow, pages
531–534 in your text." The assignment should run, "Pages
531–534 in your text consider the Protestant Reformation in
Germany. Today we have considered the Protestant Reformation
in England. You will find that Martin Luther's objections to the
Church were quite different from those of Henry VIII. I want
you to be able to tell me exactly how they were different. You
may skip the two paragraphs dealing with Calvin since we will
take them up at another time." Here the teacher has indicated
*what* he wants done. The students have an assignment. They
know *what* to do. Explaining *what* to do in the long range assignment is equally important. A teacher assigning a term paper
should be prepared to spend at least a period on spelling out
the details of his assignment, and, in most cases, should provide
each student with a written guide sheet. To assign a "book
review" is not enough. Any interested student will ask "what's a
book review?" I've been present in classrooms in which the
teacher was unable to answer definitively. He deserves what he
gets, even if it's nothing.

The second question to be treated in any homework assignment is *how* to do it. This question has obvious implications for
the long range assignment, but equally important ones for such
daily assignments as the illustrations above. The instructor who
assumes that his students can read runs grave risk of disappointment even at the graduate level. They must be taught to skim

read, to analyze and to interpret. They must be taught to recognize topical sentences and subheadings. Some students can read even chapter headings and be totally unaware of what to expect from what follows. They read all the words in a paragraph, close their eyes, and can't give the sense of what they've read.

In the instance of the long-range assignment, such as the term paper, one of the teacher's main concerns is with indicating the sources to which the student can go to fulfill the requirements of the assignment. He cannot assume that the skills involved in constructing a formal paper, or a book review, or in preparing a debate or a panel discussion develop in the student automatically. Nor can he justify his nonchalance by calling it "independent study." Students need instruction in locating sources, note taking, criticism of sources, marshalling evidence and the mechanics of synthesis. Normally, class time must be earmarked for such instruction.

The third question to be considered in giving an assignment is *when;* when the work should be done and when completed. The setting of a due date is not really as random a thing as might appear. The time allotted for the completion of the task should be an indication of the importance of the project, and an indication of the teacher's expectation as to its degree of difficulty. By the instalment plan, the teacher clearly indicates his expectations of his students. To assign a due date off-handedly for next January gives no indication as to how much work is involved. Students expect to do the paper in a week and they feel that the teacher is making the same supposition. The teacher should establish a due date that will give him plenty of time to evaluate the results carefully. For me this means the day *before* a long holiday is preferable to a due date following the holiday. Here the teacher's interest and that of his students conflict for obvious reasons. Most students get little done during a holiday (despite their most sincere and heroic intentions), so that I have not been remorseful in satisfying myself.

An adjunct to the *when* question is the consideration of what to do about late papers. The answer varies from teacher to teacher and is really a philosophical question. There seem to be three basic responses to the student's presenting his work late; flat refusal to accept it, accept it with penalty, and accept it gratefully. The teacher who flatly refuses to accept a late paper feels that by so doing he accomplishes something. This may be so. The question that comes to mind is whether the important thing is to teach punctuality or to teach what is inherent in the student's execution of the paper. While I personally do appreciate this teacher's action, I can't reconcile that action with what I would consider to be a more functional objective. If I set an assignment, it does have a purpose, and I feel that the student gains something by carrying it out—late or not. To me this is the overriding consideration. Nor will I hold a student to a due date who submits earnestly that he can meet my deadline, but could turn in better work if given a stay. I want to see the best he has to offer—nothing less.

The second teacher accepts with penalty. This, too, is somewhat difficult to justify. It raises the question of whether we're evaluating the work, or the amount of time it took. Different people work at different paces. Is it any more logical to set a grade that reflects a penalty for lateness, than it is to subtract peaches from pears? Hemingway drafted *The Sun Also Rises* in six weeks. Other novels have taken him longer. Does this become our basis of evaluation? The idea of establishing a rate of discount in terms of days late leaves me bewildered.

The third teacher who accepts the paper with a smile is censured by colleagues who claim that he has in effect penalized the kids who met the deadline. I'm not sure that this is true, nor am I sure that equity is that simple an arrangement. The answer is that the teacher must come to terms with his own value system and do whatever that system dictates. What *is* his purpose? I still set due dates and then maintain an unheralded flexibility in order to get what I want.

The question of *why* the assignment is to be done is at least as important as the first three, though it is often ignored by teachers—largely, I suspect, because they're not always clear on the matter themselves. The teacher must be so convinced as to the importance of the assignment (this includes the daily assignment) that he is able to communicate its importance to his students. The students should always be told *why* they are to do the work, and in no uncertain terms. It is of immense practical value that they know why. Usually telling them *why* takes the form of explaining how their homework relates directly to what is to be done, and the student who understands what that relationship is understands each more clearly, and the value of his effort is thereby multiplied.

In the case of the daily homework assignment, the teacher may find that anywhere from five to ten minutes is required for the giving of an effective assignment and explaining *why* it is to be done. Contrary to the teacher's immediate objection, such time is not only expendable, it is well spent. The homework assignment should be carefully introduced to the class in much the same way that a lesson has a carefully planned introduction. If the text reading to be assigned has to do with Martin Luther, then before the assignment is given, there should be a deliberate attempt to awaken an interest in Martin Luther. With the day's lesson on Henry VIII concluded, the teacher might raise some discussion as to whether or not Henry's opposition to the church was the foundation of the entire Protestant revolt. Or he might read a dramatic excerpt from Roland Bainton's *Here I Stand*. It is important that the student's interest be awakened before the assignment is made. Ideally, the student should *want* the assignment. Ideally, he should leave the class anxious to get started on his homework. Day after day, this is a great deal to expect, but the interested teacher can go a long way toward the ideal with a little effort. The veteran teacher will snigger at this, but he should give it a try, not once but over and over. I know teachers who pride themselves (and rightfully so) on making their students *want* to do it—senior high school teachers as well as junior. If you're as good as you'd like to be, can you make even the textbook come alive? I've even resorted, in the case of textbook assignments, to having the class make note of the single most asinine statement contained in the reading. Next day we compared notes discussing the reasons behind the various choices.

While we're on the subject, it's a good idea for the teacher to be somewhat discriminating in his use of the textbook (and a textbook, unfortunately, is what most of us use). The teacher is wise to deliberately skip passages or even chapters, suggesting to his class that the ideas contained therein are too nonsensical to be worthy of their attention. Chances are that they've discovered this for themselves, but the teacher's saying it provides a tremendous boost to morale.

Whether he makes a formal assignment or not, the teacher should never let up on encouraging his students to read. He does this by continually alluding to exciting ideas that he has found in his own reading, deliberately introducing books in his class and reading dramatic excerpts from them, introducing the author as an exciting rebel, taking his students on trips to paperback book shops (the school library somehow isn't the same thing), and providing for each unit reading lists of carefully selected books that he *knows* they will *enjoy*. He might set aside class time for book discussions or organize clubs for the purpose after school. I once conducted what I called a seminar in advanced nonsense after school in which we bounced from book to book in sheer delight. Students should be encouraged to read, not forced, but *sold*. It may stay with them for a lifetime. If it does, the teacher has accomplished a great thing, whether they know the date of Agincourt or not. Teachers should offer books as a *joy* (I'm opposed to book review assignments, and book reports are unspeakable). Students should be discouraged from thinking that reading is a chore. One English teacher of my acquaintance charged his students to read "either a novel, or two short novels," thus most effectively promoting exactly the wrong attitude. The more appropriate teacher gambit should be, "Here's a book you might enjoy— If you don't care for it, throw it out and get another. Life is too short to waste on dull books." Nor should a book be presented as a complete entity. I have instructed a class to read Chapter I of Robert Ardrey's *African Genesis* as particularly exciting. All of this goes on without formal assignment. Books don't belong to teachers. They belong to the people who delight in reading them. Who is a teacher to *force* someone to read, any more than to *force* him not to read?

Moving back to the formal assignment, let us say a few words on the final consideration of checking to be sure that homework is being done. To begin with, *all* homework must be checked. The teacher who has given an assignment with a purpose finds that he wants to (or at least has to) check it. This he need not be told. More than this, it must be checked immediately. Homework returned to students weeks or even days after they have completed it has little instructional value. I have found that the daily written assignment has little value in a history course. The experience of others, I assume, might contradict this. I have been faced with the task on a Tuesday night of correcting 150 homework papers which sat on my desk untouched and were joined by 150 more for Wednesday. The Tuesday pile might as well be thrown into the waste basket. After a while the absurdity of this venture dawned upon me and I convinced myself that history was primarily a reading course, not a writing course. I abandoned daily written assignments since I had neither the time nor the strength to do a proper job. Spot checking of written assignments was not a satisfactory solution.

Reading assignments are easily checked, and I have found that students will most willingly exchange the daily written work for reading with the ever present threat of a quiz on that reading. Reading assignments, too, must be checked frequently, however irregularly. Students must not be permitted to come to class unprepared or to fall behind. Insuring that they are not unprepared may require as many as three "Pearl Harbor" quizzes per week. A crackerjack biology teacher who befriended me in my first year of teaching introduced me to his own system of the postage stamp quiz. At the beginning of class, each student is provided with a slip of paper about the size of a regular postage stamp, on which he is told to number from one to five short answer questions based upon the reading assigned to his class The teacher reads them carefully and slowly, but only once. The theory behind the tiny size of the paper is that, since one thumb is required to hold it still, "academic cooperation" is brought to an *impasse*. The writing is small enough as to be read only by the student doing it. Five batches of quizzes can be carried easily in a shirt pocket, each with a paper clip. They are marked and recorded in less than half an hour. The teacher concerned with saving paper can line out the original quiz answers and present the reverse side for the next day.

The postage stamp quiz also fits well into an extremely satisfactory grading system. I have preferred to place greater emphasis upon daily preparation than upon major exams—as much as 75 per cent. If the student is to earn 75 per cent of his six weeks' grade on the quizzes, I make sure that he gets 75 questions (or 15 quizzes) over the course of the marking period. If he gets five of five correct on the first quiz he then has five of his seventy-five marks. The system works on an accumulation basis which does away with tedious averaging. In addition, the student always knows exactly where he stands. It's a *positive* grading system and eminently more satisfactory than the system more generally in use wherein the teacher *deducts* for wrong answers. The procedure here is to *add* up the right answers. The absolute beauty of the system is that the responsibility for doing the assignment and doing it well *is on the student* where it should be. If he misses a quiz because of absence, he is down five possible points and it is up to *him* to make it up or not as he chooses. Under this system, students welcome bonus questions and extra quizzes given out of the kindness of the teacher's heart. They work harder and they have a positive attitude toward homework and learning. Responsibility for learning is off the teacher and on the student where it belongs, and he has no one to blame or congratulate but himself. The teacher merely keeps the record of his successes.

# ELEVEN

## THE NASTY BUSINESS
## OF TESTING AND EVALUATION

Among the most vexatious aspects of classroom teaching is that
to the teacher's task of instruction is added the task of evaluating the students' progress. The task of evaluating is recognized by any teacher as burdensome, true enough, but more
than this the teacher will soon realize that the whole idea of
evaluating diminishes or entirely offsets the effectiveness of instruction. Evaluation corrupts instruction. The two processes
have very different ends and, worse yet, the ends are largely
exclusive of one another. When the form of evaluation is testing,
the apparent disadvantage is that time allotted to the testing is
usually time taken away from instruction. Were this the only
problem, or even the major one, the difficulty would be easily
resolved by making the academic year somewhat longer. But
the time consideration is *not* the major difficulty. The real
problem is much more significant.

The differences of ends or purposes is the great bugaboo.
When the examination is imposed upon the course of instruction, the whole intent of instruction is shifted from the personal
gratification of the human being, the satisfaction of his natural
need to learn, together with the attendant development of his

intellect, to the successful satisfaction of a perfectly artificial device. Learning becomes a chore rather than a natural recreation; an odium rather than a pleasure. The student who must prepare for an examination must adopt a posture toward learning that is both unrealistic and irrational. The new posture assumes that knowledge has little of any value in itself but is rather a negotiable instrument. Learning thus becomes a means, not an end. Curiosity or the joy of intellectual satisfaction is sublimated and, in the instance of most instruction offered in our high schools and universities, disappears completely. The major problem is a problem of artificial motivation. When the natural desire to learn is destroyed by being submerged in this way, there is little, if any, attempt to restore it. The more sensitive student consoles himself with the hope that once his schooling is finished—the evaluation over with—he will be free to begin his learning. This very idea of working off an indenture remained with me until I had completed a doctorate. Learning had nothing to do with *me*—it was a process that involved only my examiners. I had to wait for my turn—my opportunity. But the schools must provide that opportunity. They do not. For most of us, the twelfth year is the end of all that nonsense. And then we go out to work without ever having been exposed to the joy of learning; and we live out our lives (or our half lives) having passed or failed the examination. The net result of this enslavement of man to knowledge is failure. T. S. Eliot framed the tragedy beautifully when he asked, "Where is the wisdom we have lost in knowledge? Where is the knowledge we have lost in information?" *

Perhaps if there were such a thing as a perfect evaluative device that would correspond identically with what we have learned, the fundamental antagonism between the two would

---

* T. S. Eliot, "Choruses from the Rock" in *Poems 1909–1962* (New York: Harcourt, Brace & World, Inc., 1952), p. 96.

be totally resolved. It is not necessary here to state that there
are no such devices. Nor are such devices, for all the painstaking preparation, possible. Is a grade of 60% on a European
history final examination any indication that I have command
of 60% of European history? Or 90%? Or 30%? Is an average
of all my test marks a reliable index to what I have learned, or
of what there is to know? Is the mark an indication even of
my interest in the subject? Obviously not. Then why do we
pretend that it is? We pretend that it is for the sake of expediency, to have some means of classifying the learners. But
for the sake of expediency we are sacrificing education. We are,
as teachers and examiners, withholding the experience of learning from countless numbers of men and women who are
entitled by birthright to it.

Tosh and piffle, we teachers realize all this. We also are
pointedly aware of what the answer is. Few among us are opposed to the idea of abandoning the grading system. With the
grades go the evaluative devices. Several universities have
adopted the measure in one form or another. Many have maintained a strict Pass-Fail basis of evaluating for years. Of course
the evaluation of learners persists even in such systems, but the
sting of artificiality has been largely removed; and the learner
has been effectively released into a much broader world of self-
edification. He has been accorded thereby the position of master
rather than slave to the subjects he studies. Let the matter rest
with suggesting that total abandonment of grades and evaluation
is the ideal commensurate with effective learning. Twenty years
hence the practice of examining will be seen to be as barbarous
as the practice of bloodletting appears to today's surgeon.

One of the serious social problems created by our adherence
to the importance of grades is the problem of "cheating." Our
most venerable institutions on the North American continent
have not escaped the consequences, even under the so-called

"honor system." It is time for us to take a long hard look at the causes of cribbing. I believe that the spread of such practices are inevitable under the circumstances. In my experience as a high school and university instructor, the phenomenon of cheating is widespread. While estimates are hazardous, I would venture the guess that less than half of our students in high school and university have had no connection with it— either receiving or willingly giving information on examinations. Copying homework is one of the few purposeful activities of the average study hall. The world is still not in love with the cheater, but they'll soon have to make room for him. We have reached the point where an hour-long examination can affect the entire life of the student. This is a pressure that is hitherto unknown in our education system. If we are willing to reward the successful test score without concern for the learner, then we will have to readjust some of our definitions of morality. I can remember my teachers saying that the cheater only cheats himself. Granting that this may have been true once, is it true today? It is we who have emphasized that schooling is necessary to getting ahead, to getting the right job. And what is schooling? Schooling is getting good grades on the examination. It is we who, through a systematic emphasis of evaluation and testing, have de-emphasized the importance of learning in itself. It is we who, rather than insisting upon the integrity of learning and encouraging it for the joy of itself, have identified success with the satisfactory completion of exams. Which sixteen-year-old wants to face a life at the gas pump in exchange for a moral integrity which we, as teachers, believe to be of secondary importance? We have done our job well. Our students believe in the importance of examinations—their paramount importance.

To turn from the abstract considerations of the problems of testing and evaluation, let us consider the evaluative devices themselves, and their most effective execution under the circumstances which we as teachers confront. Given the situation as it stands, exams can be set and administered in such a way as to maximize their usefulness—or to minimize their uselessness, whichever. One of the basic disadvantages of the examination is that as the number of those to be examined increases, its tendency to penalize the more intelligent also increases. The principal factor involved here is that of time limitation. The true-false item is the classic illustration of this theory in effect—handled with nonchalance or on first impulse by the average or slower student, and giving pause to the more advanced student. I have found that honors students had to be "unlearned" in preparation for an examination on a state-wide basis—in this case, the New York State Regents exam in American History. The average student quickly identifies John C. Calhoun as the least "nationalistic" in a multiple choice item that includes Andrew Jackson, Henry Clay and Daniel Webster. The honors student who has read Arthur Schlesinger Jr., Richard Current and Margaret Coit wants more time. He is disadvantaged. Such students must be taught to react "instinctively" rather than intellectually. This bespeaks a poorly-set examination. Broadening the content base, as in the case of the newer New York State Comprehensive Examination in Social Studies does not substantially improve the device, which continues to seek the instinctive, rather than the thought-out response to a problem. On the first page of the June, 1968 examination, four of the nine multiple choice items begin: "Which is the most valid . . . , Which is the most valid conclusion . . . , Which is the best example . . . , and Which best supports. . . ." The stem wording suggests that more than one of the distractors is plausible, and yet only *one* can be considered correct. In short, *too much* thinking gets the student into trouble. The honor student is confronted with the need to express qualifications, that is to justify his or her choice. It is the time factor that most seriously handicaps the examinee who knows what he is doing, or thought he did. For the more reliable evaluation of learners, time should *not* be a factor. Unhappily, it is generally the chief factor. There are two apparent ways of ruling out the artificial time factor.

The first method of equalizing the time factor is the setting of a contract essay examination. Let us assume, for purposes of illustration, that the unit exam is set with three essay questions. The contract idea allows the student to elect to answer all three at 33% each, any two at 50% each, or only one upon which answer rests the full weight of the grade. Thus provision has been made in the latitude of selection for the student who has a general knowledge of the entire area, the student who feels that he can handle a major part of the area with some aplomb, and the student who can attack a particular topic convincingly, that is, bring to bear his outside reading on the subject. The student thus classifies himself in terms of his own learning and reflects at the same time his interest in the area.

A variation of the contract exam is the setting of self-determining questions. The teacher sets perhaps three questions of graduating difficulty and labels the "passing" (information) question, the "good" (understanding) question, and the "honors" (application of understanding or bibliography) question. The student is free to undertake whichever he can handle, again classifying himself. In such an evaluation, the teacher necessarily sets a ceiling, but no floor. If the student elects the "good" question, the perfect answer achieves no more than a "B." He has contracted for a "B". If he fails to answer the question satisfactorily, he is liable to failure. The contract examination, in either case, allows for the differences among students, allows for the reward of the conscientious, and relieves the examiner from having to explain to the disappointed student why a good bobcat is not equal to a lion. Generally, students define themselves quite precisely and, of course, they must be satisfied with their own definition. The beauty of the contract examination, apart from relieving the teacher of the need for justifying marks, is that it is contrived to reward the interested student who chooses to move beyond the test requirement and satisfy himself. In either case, of course, the examination questions must be very carefully prepared.

The second method of eliminating the artificial time factor is the replacement of the examination with the requirement of a position paper. The contract element may still obtain in the student's election of topics. The preparation of a paper on some aspect of the unit, *theoretically* done at leisure, permits greater opportunity for the student to reveal his interest and talent in a given subject area. For many teachers the unit position paper has replaced the examination altogether as an evaluative device. My own study, *American History and Conflicting Interpretations,* (New York: Teachers College Press, 1969) may prove useful as an illustration. Here the teacher provides, at the beginning of the unit, a carefully selected list of topics that have a relevance to the unit. The student initials his choice from the list. The teacher should provide at least the number of topics as he has members of his class and should accept alternate proposals from his students. The preparation of such a list of research topics requires that the teacher be thoroughly familiar with the resources available in the school or public library. One way of acquainting himself with the resources available is an assignment in bibliography on a given subject in which students are required to compile a list of sources on a subject without recourse to anything but the available library facilities. The assignment provides a worthwhile experience for students and a reservoir of information for the teacher upon which to build further assignments.

We have emphasized above that *theoretically* the student has more time to demonstrate his interest and talent on the position paper than he does on the exam. We know, from experience, that the preparation of a paper is often done at the last minute the day before the assignment is due. It would seem that the time factor still plagues the teacher. Such is not the case when there is careful planning. Properly, the preparation of a paper is done in a series of stages. The wise teacher does not assign a topic, a due date, and then accept the finished paper on that date. Rather, he insists on instalments, thus forcing the student through the step-by-step process of creating a respectable piece of work, and, at the same time, emphasizing the importance of each of those steps. The teacher sets a series of due dates, each corresponding to a step in the development of a worthwhile paper. The first problem of the student who has selected a topic is the definition of terms of his topic. He must identify precisely the problem at hand. The teacher wisely appoints a date upon which the student's definition of problem is due, this and nothing more. The second step is the gathering of appropriate sources, and this tentative bibliography is due on a later date. On a third date the teacher reviews the outline of the paper and perhaps the evidence that has been collected.

It is important and necessary that students—high school and graduate—be held to their topics, and extraneous material weeded out early. On a fourth date the teacher receives an evaluation of the evidence presented, that is, a specific statement as to its reliability. He next receives a rough draft of the synthesis. Finally, the teacher accepts the final draft of the position paper. At this point, it is probably worth reading and, of course, the student is pointedly aware of the process of creating a position paper. A teacher who labors over a student's paper prepared the night before the due date deserves the torment. Ordinarily the student has gained nothing in such a process. The instalment plan offers the student a genuine learning experience and the teacher a possibility of some worthwhile reading. In any event, the evaluation of what the student can do is more genuine.

The principal reason for the ineffectiveness of the essay examination as an evaluative device is carelessness—carelessness of the teacher in setting the question, and carelessness of the student in answering the question. In order to construct an effective essay examination, the teacher must give judicious consideration to the objectives and proceed with the construction of the examination only after his objectives have been carefully defined and set down on paper beforehand. The examination must be planned with the same thoroughness with which he would map out a lesson or unit plan. More often than not exam questions are set hastily with the most perfunctory concern for objectives and, therefore, without any particular design. As in lesson planning the teacher must have first, a fixed idea of exactly what point or points he wants to be brought out; and second, he must chart precisely the means for bringing out these and no others. To be sure that he has done what he thinks or hopes he has done, the teacher also constructs the model answer. A colleague reading the model answer should be able to re-construct the question in fairly close detail without having seen it. The practice has obvious merit and should be urged upon all teachers. It pays off handsomely in making the examination a useful learning experience as well as a more effective evaluative device, and it makes the marking of papers considerably less of a chore.

Unfortunately, many teachers confront a student's examination paper without knowing *exactly* what he himself wants or expects. This increases the subjectivity of his evaluation and makes the process of evaluating a positive torment. He finds himself re-reading papers already evaluated, and he is naturally (and correctly) uncomfortable with the apparent unreliability of each evaluation. He knows that he is unable to justify the grade clearly and convincingly if he should be pressed to do so—and, of course he often is. Probably the teacher's irresolution is the most hellish aspect of testing. It is completely unnecessary and is avoided with care and forethought. Student responses to well-constructed essay questions provide also, of course, a useful evaluation of his teaching. Disappointing results on a large scale indicate to him, when he knows his exam was good, the specific areas in which his teaching may have been inadequate.

But generally poor results on a carefully-set examination may be the consequence of another problem. It is readily discernible in reading the disappointing papers whether the teaching has been faulty, or the students did not respond in the area and manner prescribed by the exam. Many unsatisfactory exams are turned in by students who have ignored the questions set by the examiner, set up their own instead and have then proceeded to answer them. This is infuriating. Again, care and preparation will minimize the difficulty. Teachers, high school or university, who intend to make use of essay-type examinations, must devote time and patience to teaching their students how to take such exams—almost as an adjunct to the course. Many students who fail exams do so not because they can't handle the answers, but rather because they can't handle the questions. Even where teachers have indicated clearly and specifically what it is they want done, students mis-read questions. Part of the difficulty is that students prepare for anticipated questions and then, faced with the teacher's question, undertake to reconstruct it in terms of their own preparation. Much of this sort of thing can be obviated by distributing ahead of time either the actual exam or a list of questions from which the exam questions will be selected. Many teachers balk at the idea, feeling that a really successful evaluation of the student depends on sneaking up on him or even shocking him. Some consider the exam some sort of penal device. Their concern for what the student is learning seems to be minimal. Part of this psychology, I suppose, is the need to satisfy some curve. Sometimes we become so obsessed with distributions, with "separating the men from the boys," that we leave off our principal commitment of trying to turn as many of our boys as possible into men.

Before the teacher begins his instruction on how to write essay answers, he must be certain that students can read essay questions. Rarely is it feasible, at any level, to assume that they already know how. Students must be taught to read and re-read the question and then to break the question down into its component parts and to consider how each part is distinct and how each is related to the other parts. When distinguishing the component parts of a question, it is useful to have a pencil in hand and to use it. One of the reasons that students have difficulty in following instructions is that they do not distinguish the meaning of words carefully, or when they do take the trouble to define for themselves what such words as "discuss," "explain," "relate," or "show how" mean, their own conception differs from that of their examiners. Often they lump all such words of instruction together and read them as "snow me." Both the examiner and his examinees must be aware of the difference between the questions that read "give three results of the defeat of the Spanish Armada," and "Show how the defeat of the Spanish Armada had lasting results in European development." The former is a particularly poor question in that it is first, a simple recall question and not an essay question at all (better to have been framed as a multiple choice item), and second, because it does not channel the student sufficiently into producing any significant answer. Two students who respond respectively, "It weakened Spain by making Dutch independence possible, paved the way to the accession of Henry IV in

France, and established maritime hegemony for England," and "It gladdened the heart of Elizabeth I, again brought Drake's seamanship to the attention of the English, and caused much rotting of timber at the bottom of the English Channel," have each satisfied the terms of the question. Probably they have not both satisfied the teacher's expectation. He would probably grade the first higher and the second lower (and seemingly rightly enough), but could he justify such a thing on the basis of his question?

To answer the "show how" (latter) question, the student would have to move further than recall into demonstrating the relationship between the triumph of a Protestant power and the accession of Henry IV. If the teacher wants this particular connection developed, he must set this into his question—*not assume* that the student will discuss the Armada in terms of the French Civil War. The only sound evaluation of the student's understanding rests squarely upon his knowing exactly what he is to do. Carefully structured questions do *not* reduce the student's latitude for independent thought, though often the teacher seizes upon this as a rationale for his carelessly ambiguous questions. Having to mark the papers becomes his own retribution. If he has sown the wind, let him inherit the whirlwind. But the students suffer meanwhile, and the opinion spreads in the faculty rooms that they are stupid. The fact is not, however, that they're stupid, but that they didn't guess right. This is the teacher's fault. He's stupid or doesn't care.

If the teacher is disposed to distribute his examination topics ahead of time, to provide take-home exams, or to make use of the open-notes exam, he might satisfy himself further by removing the device entirely from the examination category characterized by multiple questioning and more stringent time limitations and adjust himself comfortably to the fact that he is requiring something other than an exam in the common sense of the word as an evaluative device. He has moved in the direction of assigning a position paper, and is willing to focus his evaluation on what his student can do with both time and sources available to him. The position paper, apart from what might be construed as a disadvantage of examining the students' competence in only one area, has several compensating advantages. Preference for one over the other reflects his basic view of what is of greater importance in teaching social studies and what of lesser. Certainly the teacher operating on the basis of the paramount importance of coverage is not disposed toward abandoning the exam. Since this is not my own persuasion, I serve up few exams and rely heavily upon the students' preparation of formal papers. Like effective examinations, however, effective position or term papers must be very carefully constructed. Perhaps the best way to illustrate what goes into such construction is to consider, Aquinas-fashion, the objections to papers and then to try to answer them. Teachers' aversion to using term papers coincide largely with student dislike of them, and we will treat them in terms of the common student complaints.

The most general objection seems to be that papers are "busy work" especially among university students where papers are in much wider use. Almost all professors are strangely obsessed with the notion that a course must have a paper. In so many instances the objection that papers are "busy work" are 100% correct. A professor in a survey course on German history requires a paper of each of his students though the student may or may not have either earlier work or interest in German history. Obviously, if the student doesn't read any German, the paper he produces must be a synthesis, or worse a compilation, of secondary sources and translations. Equally obvious then, the paper produced cannot possibly have any value as an original communication. In these terms, my own position is that there is enough bad history being written by professionals interested in the subject, without students—high school, undergraduate or graduate—adding liberally to the tonnage. Most students who are being driven into writing by course requirements should, in fact, be *discouraged* from writing. When the student has some background *and an idea* he should approach his instructor, or be approached by his instructor, to discuss the idea and the possibility of writing on it. No paper should be produced by a student whose interest is solely in the satisfaction of a course requirement. Teachers who assign them on this basis are poetically punished by having to read them.

When the student is genuinely interested in a topic then he may write, and he derives both formative and informative value from doing so. In order to derive informative value from preparing a paper he must begin with a *question*. If he is seriously interested in answering the question for *himself*—rather than in satisfying the teacher—his approach to the subject will be thorough and critical enough so that a formative value accrues as well. It doesn't happen automatically. He must be guided in the method of his discipline. I'm not at all sure that assigning papers on the single ground of an exercise in the discipline is appropriate to public education. Most students in our social studies classes do not go on to become professional historians or social scientists. If they do, they will be properly equipped in the course of their special training to carry out research. The idea of assigning term papers in high school so that students are prepared to do them in college leaves me absolutely cold. In assigning a written paper, then, the teacher must have carefully weighed his objectives, know exactly why he is assigning the paper in terms of his subject area and of his students, and be able to explain these objectives to them so that they are convinced. This is a tall order. I submit that anything less, however, is a waste of time and energy the net result of which is student exasperation and several pounds of trash for the teacher to read *and evaluate.*

A second objection, related directly to the first, is that the topics are "stupid." From what has been said above, it is imperative that the teacher tailor the assigned topic to the personal interest of the student. It is useful to have the individual student indicate an area of interest and then to devise a topic based upon his indicated preference. Needless to say, every student should have his own topic. It is also useful to have them elect this topic from a number of possibilities in the chosen area. In allowing this latitude in student choice, however, the teacher must guard against the possibility of the student's having a ready-made paper provided by an older brother who had done it in college.

Another reason why students identify a topic as "stupid," is that it's too broad. It is important that he have something manageable to work with that he can get his teeth into. The teacher must see to it that his student does not settle down to confront a topic such as "Peter the Great," or "The American Revolution," or "The British Postal System," or "The Civil Rights Problem." They may accept the topic fervently enough but of course they soon find that they can't come to grips with it, and after writing the first line, the fervor dwindles into exasperation and defeat. Even "Peter the Great and the Westernization of Russia" is broad enough to give a professional some concern the rest of his lifetime. "Was it necessary for Peter to execute his own son?" is interesting enough to gain the student's attention, narrow enough to allow him to focus that attention, and moot enough to allow him some latitude in defining his problem and attacking it with some originality, and personal satisfaction. Of course, what he learns of the character of absolutism, the nature of Peter or of the Romanovs or Czars in general, the paternal instinct, the circumstances of revolution, the human response to oppression, and so on, are all built into the carefully-chosen topic. This topic is not "stupid." The importance of the student's work is enhanced if use can be made of it in class. Though not for a moment would we urge the teacher to indulge in a general reading of all papers before the class. This is deadly. The one thing that a student does not care to listen to is a series of reports prepared by his fellow students for several days running. Better the teacher should talk than this.

A third major objection to term papers involves the time element. The paper is assigned in September of one year and collected in January of the next. The student does the whole thing in the two days before the due date. He was interested in September, went to the library on the day the paper was assigned and then not again for three months. In the meanwhile the paper becomes a Damocletian sword. The impact is the same as getting a football team "up" for a game Saturday, and then having the game postponed. Disappointing results in papers are usually attributable to the students' having had too much time rather than too little. They rarely protest having too much time but do plead "not enough." The problem is that they, like us, do things at the last minute. For this reason and for several other obvious reasons, the teacher is wise to use the instalment plan of accepting papers. This allows him to underscore the distinct steps involved in the preparation of a useful paper, to apportion allotted time in accord with student requirements, and to direct students in their work step-by-step from the beginning. At intervals of one or two weeks, he can call for the student's statement in defining his problem (and make whatever adjustments necessary to avoiding weeks of wasted work), a tentative bibliography (whereby he acquaints himself and student with the sources that are available), a tentative outline of the paper (where he can weed out irrelevancies and propose omitted considerations), student notes (and provide instruction on the proper taking of such), student criticism of the sources (introducing the student to the question of reliability of sources), and the final draft which, at that point, should be more worth reading. Certainly by the time the student applies himself to the task of writing the final draft, it should be much easier.

A fourth major objection that students raise is that their work is evaluated on a quantitative rather than qualitative basis. The instalment plan diminishes this possibility. In addition, teachers must be careful to avoid specifying length. Usually this is the first question that students ask, "How long should it be?" How can one tell? Yet professors and teachers both blithely appoint that it shall be "2500 words," or perhaps "Ten typewritten pages," ("Twenty" if it's a graduate student.) Teachers should require that students pay attention to format, to consistency in footnoting and bibliography but should not emphasize this as many of us are fond of doing. Teachers and students easily become preoccupied with margins when more substantive considerations are impossible. Rather, the teacher should be emphasizing the originality and care with which the subject has been handled. Another artful device is for the teacher to have students exchange papers and correct them. The teacher already knows, from his instalment plan, the calibre of work that the student is doing, and the correction of mechanics and content by fellow students is generally very thorough.

A final major plea of the student whose work is unsatisfactory is that he "couldn't find anything on the topic." The instalment plan corrects for this possibility too. In addition, the teacher is wise to provide a thorough introduction of his students to the library and its use, and to provide when necessary, further additional help on an individual basis. Perhaps some class time can be spent in the library effectively.

Exam or paper, the teacher through careful planning and execution, provides an evaluation of his students that is both useful to his students and to himself.